Aladd ... TH ...

A Pantomime

John Morley

Samuel French - London
New York ...

CHARACTERS

Aladdin Twankey, a Chinese Laundry Boy
Widow Twankey, a Chinese Washerwoman, his mother
Wishee Washee Twankey, another Laundry Boy, his brother
The Great Abanazar, the wicked Egyptian Magician
Chopsuey the Twelfth, Emperor of China
Dragona the Thirteenth, his wife and Empress
Princess Say Wen, their daughter
So Shi, her Handmaiden
Sing Hi, another Handmaiden
Chow Mien, the Grand Vizier
Prince Pekoe, his son
Bamboo ⎱
Typhoo ⎰ Chinese Police
Rick Shaw, a lady Taxidriver
Strong Pong, the Emperor's dreaded Executioner
Madam Flash Bang, the royal Photographer
Mazda, the Genie of the Lamp
Mazawattee, the Spirit of the Ring
The Egyptian Mummy
Chinese Citizens, Attendants at Abanazar's Magic Show, Customers at the Laundry, the Spirits of the Cave, Diners at the Flied Lice Inn, Egyptian Slaves, Guests at the Wedding Feast

NOTE: the two Chinese Police can be male or female, and are equally effective, if less usual, as "Two Chinese Policewomen"

ACT I

ACT II

NOTE: The scenes move straightforwardly between full set, front cloth, full set, front cloth, etc. They can be made spectacular, but the front cloth scenes are just as effective in terms of comedy and story if simply played in front of tabs

SUGGESTIONS FOR MUSICAL NUMBERS

The songs suggested here are based on audience research, for pantomime audiences like to hear the songs they know. You are, of course, welcome to alter the choice of songs but it is most important to note that a licence issued by Samuel French Ltd to perform the pantomime does not include permission to use any copyright songs or music. The notice issued by the Performing Right Society (and printed on page vi) should be read most carefully.

ACT I

Song 1	Chinatown	Courtiers
Song 2	For Once In My Life	Aladdin and Courtiers (production number)
Song 3	Hey, Look Me Over	Twankey (and perhaps Courtiers)
Song 4	If It Takes For Ever	Princess and Handmaidens
Song 4(a)	The Old Bazaar in Cairo	Incidental music for Abanazar's Magic Show
Song 5	That Old Black Magic	Aladdin and Citizens
Song 6	Chinese Limehouse Laundry Blues	Twankey, Wishee, Citizens
Song 6(a)	Nellie Dean	Emperor, Empress, two Policemen
Song 7	Baubles, Bangles and Beads	Magic Cave People
Song 2	(reprise)	Aladdin

ACT II

Song 8	It's Today (from *Mame*)	Princess, Handmaidens, Citizens
Song 9	One (from *Chorus Line*)	Aladdin, Wishee, Genie, Twankey
Song 9(a)	Baubles, Bangles and Beads	Slave Girls
Song 10	Flash, Bang, Wallop	All, except Abanazar
Song 11	If I Were A Rich Man	Abanazar and Slaves of the Pyramid
Song 11(a)	"Mummy Song"	Wishee, Twankey and Aladdin
Song 12	Coming Round the Mountain (songsheet)	Twankey and Wishee
Song 1	(reprise)	Company

A licence issued by Samuel French Ltd to perform this play does NOT include permission to use any copyright music in the performance. The notice printed below on behalf of the Performing Right Society should be carefully read.

The following statement concerning the use of music is printed here on behalf of the Performing Right Society Ltd, by whom it was supplied

The permission of the owner of the performing right in copyright music must be obtained before any public performance may be given, whether in conjunction with a play or sketch or otherwise, and this permission is just as necessary for amateur performances as for professional. The majority of copyright musical works (other than oratorios, musical plays and similar dramatico-musical works) are controlled in the British Commonwealth by the PERFORMING RIGHT SOCIETY LTD, 29–33 BERNERS STREET, LONDON W1P 4AA.

The Society's practice is to issue licences authorizing the use of its repertoire to the proprietors of premises at which music is publicly performed, or, alternatively, to the organizers of musical entertainments, but the Society does not require payment of fees by performers as such. Producers or promoters of plays sketches, etc., at which music is to be performed, during or after the play or sketch, should ascertain whether the premises at which their performances are to be given are covered by a licence issued by the Society, and if they are not, should make application to the Society for particulars as to the fee payable.

Description of Characters

Aladdin: ambitious and cheeky, yet friendly. Very much in love with the Princess, and this fact "works the story".

Widow Twankey: an ever optimistic and fun-loving old girl.

Wishee Washee: like the rest of the Twankey family, ebullient and cheerful. This is really a "personality part".

The Great Abanazar: has plenty of comedy, but should remember he is a villain. If he forgets this and plays for charm, and "wanting to be liked" too much, the play suffers. He is a schemer, and it helps the telling of the story if his costume and make-up are not in any way "pantomime Chinese", but are clearly Egyptian-Arabian in style.

Chopsuey the Twelfth: the definitive henpecked husband. The part works well if he appears to be old but fruity.

Dragona the Thirteenth: the definitive wife who wears the trousers.

Princess Say Wen: is pretty but has plenty of spirit, and stands up to her parents and later to Abanazar's wicked treatment of her.

So Shi: pronounced "So Shy", and it is attractive if she, and the Princess, have stylized Oritental Chinese movements—especially So Shi.

Chow Mien, The Vizier: is ruthless, head of the Secret Police and ambitious for his son, Pekoe.

Prince Pekoe: the second Principal Boy. He enters into the fun of the story, but in some scenes is haughty and scheming. He should be played as a character part and not a vague second Principal Boy. He is, after all, Aladdin's rival. Preferably played by a female.

Strong Pong: a small part, but he causes terror.

Madam Flash Bang: is fussy, a curious Chinese lady photographer.

Bamboo: is the more intelligent of the daft Police: he is continually hitting Typhoo with a truncheon, and Typhoo fights back.

Typhoo: is a bit of an idiot.

Mazda, The Genie: needs great presence and dignity and is not to be played for comedy. He is *the story*, and must indicate this in performance.

Mazawattee, the Spirit of the Ring: she is orientally attractive, with hands held in the Hindu style, as though praying. She has presence and as her dialogue is so important—it "works the plot"—then it is best if she speaks almost every word of it directly to the audience, *not* to others on stage.

Rick Shaw: is a Chinese version of a girl mini-cab driver. She is cheerful and perky, with a "catch-phrase".

Production Notes

Abanazar's Magic Show: there need not be many people on stage watching this if they are needed as conjuring assistants. Perhaps the group watching are just the "Court", that is the **Emperor, Empress, Vizier, Princess** and **Pekoe,** who are all at a downstage corner.

Laundry Scene: the four tubs from which the items are taken can be cut-outs that look like old-fashioned tubs on legs, and behind are boxes to contain the various items of laundry.

Cave Scene: when **Abanazar** appears at the entrance he may need to hold an unseen torch that shines upwards on to his face. This solves a lighting problem, and also looks suitably sinister. It used to be traditional that **Aladdin,** when alone in the cave, had a solo song, but this is no longer possible, as the audience knows the story so well that they will shout out "Rub the lamp!" during such a solo—no matter how good a singer **Aladdin** may be.

Transformation: this may be easier to effect if the practical door to the cave is at an upstage wing, away from the backcloth.

The Magic Palace: the top edge of the ground-row representing the rooftops of Pekin and a hill needs to be fairly horizontal except for the hill itself, and to be about 3 feet high to allow a manipulator to work behind it without being seen by the audience. Later in the scene the **Genie** conjures up the magic palace. For this moment, the manipulator enters unseen behind the ground-row until he is behind the hill. When the **Genie** commands, the manipulator slowly lifts into view a cut-out palace and rests it on a shelf attached to the back of the hill. Thus the palace will have magically "grown out of the hill".

The magic palace cut-out is a brightly coloured cut-out of a pagoda-style building, and is about 3 foot by 3 foot. On its back is a strut so that it can stand on the shelf. When it is required to "fly away magically" the manipulator (whose arms must be the same colour as the sky of cyclorama) lifts it up into the air above, though not too high or the human arms will be noticed. The palace has at its base stylized clouds as seen in Oriental paintings, which have not been seen until this moment as they have been hidden by the "hill". The manipulator now slowly moves sideways behind the fairly horizontal collection of Pekin rooftops, holding the palace so that it appears to float across Pekin and then to disappear into the wings.

This "flying palace" business can be done more simply by nylon wires lifting it into the flies, but this way there is *no surprise* because the nylon wires can be clearly seen throughout. There are other possible scenic ideas, and perhaps UV lighting can be used: but the cut-out idea works well.

Wishee's Magic Change of Clothing (see page 41): when the **Genie** makes his magic pass at **Wishee** there is a flash in the footlights which will partly hide his removing his nightshirt and cap with the use of "velcro". Underneath the nightshirt and cap he wears a gaudy pop costume.

Twankey's Magic Change of Clothing: her costume need simply be a glittery full-length coat and hat which is like an enormous pagoda to get the effect, so this Act Two quick change is simple.

The Mummy's Costume: can be white gloves, socks and canvas shoes; a white T-shirt and tights which have bandages sewn on to them. The canvas shoes also have bandages sewn on. The head is a head mask, also covered in bandages.

Twankey's Whisky Bottle: it is important to choose a suitable type of bottle for the scene where she splashes the audience and to rehearse with it full of water. The audience should be sprinkled—not drowned.

Finale: this can open in half light to show off the lit Chinese lanterns. This is an original-looking pantomime scene, and can be very attractive. In the song-sheet before the Finale the "Willow Pattern Plate" is rolled on for a bit of fun with the audience—but the famous Pattern can be used for the Finale scenery, which would then be entirely blue and white, the scenery suggesting the bridge, trees and pagoda on the Chinese Plate. The costumes would be the same blue and white, with no other colours. Either "Lanterns" or "Willow Pattern Plate" works well for this Finale.

PROLOGUE (in Egypt)—*optional*

This is in front of the tabs, or is a frontcloth suggesting Egypt—a temple (exterior or interior) or the Sphinx itself. After the short Overture, dramatic music as the CURTAIN *rises on Abanazar,* C, *his back to the audience, waving his arms to and fro above his head. Percussion crash as he turns round and laughs fiendishly at the audience*

Abanazar Ha ha ha! I am Abanazar the wicked Egyptian magician! And this magician has an ambition! I may live here in Egypt but I want to CONQUER THE WORLD! Ha ha ha! (*As the audience reacts*) Be quiet you neurotic numbskulls that live in (local place)! Listen while I tell you how I'm going to *achieve* my ambition! (*He paces about the stage, declaiming*) You've heard of (political or television villain)? I'm *worse*!

'Cos I want to rule the Universe!
Of the whole wide world, I want to be King—
And to give me what I want, I'll rub the Magic Ring!

He rubs an impressive ring on his finger. Calling

> Spirit of the Ring, step forth!
> I want to rule the South and North
> The East and West—the whole damn lot—

There is a burst of music and a crash from percussion as the Spirit of the Ring runs in and poses, her hands held up in the Hindu style. She addresses the audience, not Abanazar

Spirit   Alas oh Master, I can *not*
Help you with your cunning deed.
The MAGIC LAMP is what you need!
Abanazar The "Magic Lamp?" Is it a toy?
Spirit   Oh no. A cheeky Chinese boy
Called Aladdin will get you the Lamp
Abanazar *Aladdin*? You mean some Chinese scamp?
But why can't *I* get the Lamp? I'm strong,
Why must I take this boy along?
Spirit   The Lamp is in a magic cave
And only Aladdin young and brave
Can enter the door. It's a magic portal
That keeps out every single mortal.
THE CAVE MUST BE ENTERED BY AN HONEST YOUTH.

Abanazar (*insincere*) Well *I'm* honest, and that's the truth!
(*He shrugs*) All right, so Aladdin must take me there
But this magic cave—where is it? *Where*?
Spirit It's high in the mountains near Pekin.
Abanazar Then now let evil magic begin!

Both Abanazar and the Spirit wave their arms about above their heads, making dramatic magic passes. There is thunder and lightning and music and Abanazar calls out over it

Abanazar Now lightning strike and thunder crash
Take me to Pekin—quick as a flash!
Spirit (*calling out over the music, making magic passes*) It shall de done, oh Master! Saleeda! Saleeda! Saleeda!
Abanazar (*also calling out and making magic passes*) Saleeda! Saleeda! Saleeda!

Percussion and dramatic music crashes out as they exit at opposite sides and the Tabs open to show Scene 1

If this optional Prologue is used then the following dialogue must be inserted between the single ruled lines on pages 11–13:

Vizier Find success! *Never!*
Abanazar (*looking up, to the audience*) I don't want to find success, I want to find the lamp! (*He returns to tidying up*)
Vizier (*conspiratorially leading Pekoe downstage*) My boy, I wish to talk with you about your future.
Pekoe My future?
Vizier Yes, you—*and the Princess.*
Pekoe But she doesn't care about me! She doesn't even *look* at me!
Vizier (*cunningly*) She will—soon. Once we break into the Cave of a Thousand Jewels up in the mountains.
Pekoe But father, nobody knows the way to open its door!
Abanazar(*looking up, to the audience*) I do! Ha ha ha! (*He returns to tidying up*)
Vizier Then we must go home and *think* of a way. (*Greatly frustrated*) How can we get into the magic cave . . . (*He looks on the floor, shaking his head with frustration*)
Pekoe Yes—how can we get into the magic cave . . . (*He looks on the floor, also shaking his head with frustration*)

And shaking their heads, scheming, they both cross the stage and exit

As they go, Abanazar addresses the audience

Abanazar All this makes my wicked heart gladden!
So now to find the boy Aladdin!
I'll soon rule the Universe, you ignorant shower,
Once I have Aladdin in my power!
Ha ha ha ha ha ha!

Abanazar exits

The Princess enters

Aladdin enters from the other side, with a bag of laundry

Aladdin (*hissing across to her*) Ssssss!

Princess Aladdin! What are you doing here?

The scene then continues as on page 13.

ACT I

Scene 1

THE COURTYARD OF THE EMPEROR CHOPSUEY'S PALACE IN PEKIN

The wings are pagoda style buildings and at the back is the grand looking pagoda style palace, perhaps in Chinese red with columns. Various banners with large Chinese letters on them.

Chinese Citizens with pigtails are already entering, trotting to and fro and bowing to each other, the girls using oriental fans. The music has become up tempo, and they sing and dance

SONG 1

After the song, the first Courtier beckons to everyone

First Courtier Hey! You know the police are after Aladdin!

All Really? Didn't know that!

Second Courtier The police are after Wishee Washee as well!

First Courtier Then we'd better warn him! Come on!

All (*calling*) Wishee! Where are you, Wishee! Wishee Washee!

They exit calling for him. As they go Wishee enters to loud, bouncey music

Wishee (*happily*) I'm Wishee Washee, Aladdin's brother! Hello, kids! (*He reacts to the few replies*) It must be Sunday. There's nobody here, I'll try again. Hello, kids!

Audience Hello!

Wishee It *is* Sunday. You must help me! I mean, when I say Hello, kids, you're supposed to say Hello, Wishee! Hello, kids!

Audience Hello, Wishee!

Wishee Beautiful. Unbelievable. You sound like Shirley Bassey singing in her bath. Let's do a bit more. Whatever I say, you say. Hello, hello!

Audience Hello, hello!

Wishee Louder! Hello, hello!

Audience Hello, Hello!

Wishee Lovely. Tickerty-boo!

Audience Tickerty-boo!

Wishee Sparkle! Sparkle!

Audience Sparkle! Sparkle!

Wishee Umpah! Umpah!

Audience Stick it up your jumpah!

Wishee (*laughing*) You got there before me, you rotten lot! Well, now we're friends I want you to do something for me. I've been growing a Chinese fruit tree down there. (*He goes to the side of the proscenium*) Chinese fruit trees are very precious and if anyone takes it, it may not grow. So will you look after it for me?

Audience Yes!

Wishee Thank you, you are kind, and we'll have a practice session. I'll pretend I'm someone else and when I go to the fruit tree you yell out "Wishee"—all right?

He whistles, walks about casually, goes up to a pot with a bit of plant showing

Audience Wishee!

Wishee Lovely. Now, I don't suppose anyone *will* go anywhere near my Chinese fruit tree but—

One of the Courtiers enters, sees the tree, goes up to it

—you never know, I mean they are quite valuable, Chinese fruit trees are . . .

Audience Wishee!

Wishee I have tried to water it with liquid manure and . . .

Audience Wishee!

Wishee I suppose it will be all right but sometimes I wonder if—what's the matter?

Audience Wishee! Man at the tree! etc.

Wishee You what? Eh? (*He sees Courtier*) Hey you, get out of it! (*He shouts and runs up to the Courtier*)

The Courtier exits

That's the idea. Don't forget to call out Wishee—oh and don't forget the other thing, when I say Hello, kids, you say Hello, Wishee, so HELLO, KIDS!

Audience Hello, Wishee!

Wishee (*waving good-bye*) Thanks! Super! 'Bye!

He exits waving

From the other side two Chinese Police (men or women) enter to vaudeville music, on scooters or skateboards, shouting. They are Superintendent Bamboo and Sergeant Typhoo

Police Aladdin! Where's Aladdin! Find Aladdin!

Bamboo I'm Superintendent Bamboo!

Typhoo And I'm Sergeant Typhoo! (*Calling to the audience*) Yoo-hoo.

Audience Typhoo!

Typhoo That's right!

Bamboo We're looking for Aladdin, we found him kissing the Princess in the Palace garden!

Typhoo When I get him, I'll say to him "Irish stew! Irish stew!"

Bamboo You're Chinese—what you shouting Irish stew for?

Typhoo Irish stew in the name of the law!
Bamboo (*hitting Typhoo with his truncheon*) You're supposed to be intelligent, you're a *policeman*.
Typhoo (*posing with arms outstretched*) I'm a tree, I'm a tree!
Bamboo What d'you mean, you're a tree? You're a policeman.
Typhoo I'm Special Branch.
Bamboo (*hitting him*) Pull yourself together.

Typhoo does actions of pulling himself together

We'll get the citizens to help us. (*He calls out*) Everybody here!

All the Citizens and Courtiers enter as Bamboo shouts at them

We've come to arrest Aladdin! He was found kissing the Princess! Where is he?
Citizens Aladdin? He's over there! Yes, that's right, over there! He went that way!

They all point off. The Police stand at attention by the scooters

> **Police** We gotta find Aladdin
> We gotta find Aladdin
> We gotta find Aladdin
> YEAH!

On the word " Yeah" they both kick up their right leg, American vaudeville style and exit with the scooters

While music starts, the Citizens run upstage to a laundry basket that has just been pushed on and open the lid

Aladdin steps out

Aladdin Hello everybody! Well, as we Chinese say, turned out rice again! My name's Aladdin! I'm in terrible trouble with the police 'cos I've parked my rick shaw on a double yellow line. I wrote rude words on the Great Wall of China . . . And now I've walked into the Palace garden and chatted up the Princess! I'm crazy about her! Yes, at last I've got somebody to live for! (*He sings*)

SONG 2

(*After the number*) I must tell my Mum about the Princess. I tell my Mum everything. I know, she'll be in The Rover's Return. (*Or some well known local pub*) Mum! Mum! Widow Twankey!

All exit calling for Twankey

She enters holding a big plastic bag or a basket

Twankey Hello, folks, I'm Widow Twankey! (*To someone in the front row*) No dear, not cranky, *Twankey*. (*To the audience*) Cheeky devil. Yes, I'm Widow Twankey and my two sons are Wishee Washee and Aladdin and we're ever so poor. (*She encourages the audience to join her when*

she says "Aah") My husband was a wonderful man, wonderful, but then
he died. (*She says "Aah" with the audience*) Poor man, he had a terrible
end—he had lumbago and we rubbed him with alcohol and he broke
his back trying to lick it off. So then I had to start a laundry. I put a
notice in the front window "Respectable young widow wants washing"
—I got some funny replies, I can tell you. My husband left me so poor
I had to put my babies in the same nappy—that's how we made ends
meet. And I couldn't afford talcum powder—my kids had to rough it.
Aladdin's the one that gets in trouble. I remember when he first sat on
the stove in the laundry and didn't feel it—I thought "Oh dear, oh dear,
he's a dead end kid". (*She laughs heartily*) He's a Dead End Kid! (*She
stops laughing*) Please yourself. He was only five when he stole a chicken
and fell foul of the law. Then one day he plugged my electric blanket into
the gas main and blew me out of bed! Still, they're lovely boys and I've
been doing the shopping at Tesco's—(*or a local supermarket*)—for them.
(*Looking in her basket*) Oh, I've bought far too much, would you like
some of it?

Audience Yes!

Twankey Well, Aladdin is very fond of music so I've bought him some
Tunes. Here you are! (*She throws packet of Tunes to the audience*) And
Wishee loves space travel so I've bought him a Mars. (*She throws it out
to the audience*) Oh, I forgot—any of you suffer from night starvation?
Then here's a packet of crisps—have a little nibble in the night! (*She
throws a packet—then a second packet which is deliberately undone, the
crisps fly all over the audience and she reacts as though it's an accident.
She laughs*) Oh dear! Someone's got a chip on her shoulder. You're
covered in them—so am I—still my dress is all right, isn't it? (*As she
shows it off she starts to sing*)

SONG 3

*She straightway gets the audience to clap in time. If required, most of the
Courtiers can join Twankey in her song and dance, instead of entering later,
which would make this a Production Number. After the song, we at once
hear a loud fanfare. Panic for Widow Twankey, she rushes to and fro*

The trumpets! It means the Emperor and Empress are coming! Help!
Good-bye! See you soon!

*Widow Twankey exits, blowing kisses, crashes into the false proscenium,
exits with more waves. We hear whistles being blown, as the Courtiers
enter in procession. Last to arrive are the two Chinese Police, now behaving
ceremonially*

Bamboo Make way for Chow Mien, the Grand Vizier of China!
Typhoo And Strong Pong, the Emperor's Executioner!

*The Vizier enters, holding a large scroll, followed by the black masked
Executioner, Strong Pong, who holds a massive sword shaped like a
scimitar*

Vizier Citizens of Pekin, and of all the Chinese Nation
         Here is the Royal Proclamation!
         Any man that looks at the Princess's face
         Shall be executed in the market place.

Strong Pong nods his head, pleased

         Or his head might be knocked off
         By a policeman's truncheon
         At twelve o'clock midday
         Just before luncheon.

The two Police nod their heads, pleased

Bamboo Kow tow! Kow tow!
Typhoo (*gormless but cheerful*) How now, kow tow!
Bamboo (*hitting him*) NOT NOW! Kow tow!

The Executioner notices the magic tree at the proscenium

Strong Pong (*with a gruff grunt*) Yang soo chang! (*He strides over to the tree at the proscenium arch*)
Audience Wishee!

Wishee enters

Wishee (*happily*) Thanks, kids! (*He comes to the tree, then sees the Executioner and is scared but defiant*) You stay away from my tree!
Strong Pong Kung Fu!
Wishee Kung Fu to you, too!

Wishee exits

Loud fanfare and music

Bamboo His Majesty, the Emperor of China—Chopsuey the Twelfth!

A couple of Attendants enter, ushering in the Emperor (a meek little man), and the Empress (a galleon in full sail)

During the following the Emperor says some of his lines aside to the audience, who are his friends

Emperor (*to the audience*) I am Chopsuey the twelfth and this is . . .
Empress (*booming*) I am Dragona the thirteenth, the Empress of China, and I'm very big in Government circles.
Emperor (*to the audience*) She's very big in other places too!

The Emperor laughs. The Empress glares at him. He stops laughing at once

Empress (*referring to the audience*) Aren't you going to acknowledge them?
Emperor (*waving to the audience*) Greetings, objects!
Empress *Subjects*. I'd better take over.
Emperor You always do, dear.
Empress I am the Empress of China and this insignificant speck of dust on a Chinese carpet is the Emperor. (*She glares at him*) Aren't you?

Emperor Yes, dear.

Empress We live in the Imperial Palace over there. (*She moves her arm round to point to it and knocks him over—percussion crash*) What are you doing down there?

Emperor Getting up.

Empress We live in Pekin. We are therefore Pekinese.

Emperor (*to the audience*) She won first prize at Crufts.

Empress What?

Emperor I said my hair is coming out in tufts. (*He takes off hat, scratches*) It's my pigtail! It's got dandruff!

Empress I don't know what you're talking about. You are two steps away from an idiot.

Emperor Then I'll move. (*He takes two steps*)

Empress Come back here. I am going to issue a decree.

Emperor What, in front of all the people?

Empress If anyone dares to look at our daughter, the beautiful Princess Say Wen, his head will be cut off.

Emperor Well, that's one way of getting a head. Hahaha . . .!

Empress Silence! I'm worried about our daughter. Men *like* to look at her. There are peeping Toms peeping, I know there are.

Emperor In Pekin. (*To the audience, enjoying himself*) There are peeping Toms peeking in Pekin, and Peeping Toms that peek in Pekin will be punished in front of the population at the peak hour.

Empress I am speakin'.

Emperor Speakin' in Pekin.

Empress If a man is found daring to look at our daughter, I will have him executed.

Emperor Step this way for the elocution!

Empress I am anxious for our dear daughter. I have qualms.

Emperor (*to the audience*) You can get pills for that!

Empress As no one is about, our daughter the Princess can arrive. (*She imperiously gestures off*) As for us, we will progress. This is a Royal Walkabout. (*She starts to exit, again brushing him aside*)

Emperor More like a Royal Knockabout! (*Chatting*) Yes, well, good-bye, everyone. It's been smashing meeting you, I've really enjoyed it, and if you want to phone me some time . . .

Empress (*booming*) CHOPSUEY!

Emperor Coming dear. (*To the audience*) You'd never believe it but I think she's ever so sexy.

The Emperor scuttles off after the Empress and all exit with them. Pretty Chinese style music is heard and two Handmaidens enter—So Shi and Sing Hi—walking with very small steps in the Chinese way and holding parasols. The Princess enters

Princess (*speaking over the music*) It is nice to escape from the palace for a while! I hate being told what to do all the time! Yes, I know I'm supposed to be marrying Prince Pekoe, but I don't love him! Oh well, I *will* find the right person for me, however long it takes! (*She sings*)

SONG 4

As she sings, her two Handmaidens stand either side of her and do stylized Chinese mime movements, and perhaps sing with her

After the song Aladdin enters loudly singing a snatch of his opening song. He sees the Princess, and stops

Aladdin Oh! The girl I met in the palace garden!
Princess You know who I am?
Aladdin (*nodding*) You're ssssh—you know who. You're my Princess!
Princess My Aladdin! But you must never speak to me!
Aladdin Rubbish!
Princess I am to marry Prince Pekoe, son of the Grand Vizier!
Aladdin Not if I have anything to do with it!
Princess If the Executioner sees you he'll chop off your head with his axe!
Aladdin Oh, I won't let a little thing like that come between us.
Princess But to risk talking to me! You must be out of your tiny Chinese mind!
Aladdin (*romantically*) I've looked up your name in the dictionary. Confucius he say, Princess Say Wen means Princess Beautiful.
Princess (*romantically*) You're very nice . . .

A trumpet fanfare sounds

(*Alarmed*) The Trumpets! You must go! It's time for my birthday celebrations!
Aladdin Then I'll see you after them!
Princess Oh yes! But now—go—please!
Aladdin Okay—but *don't worry.*
Princess I can't help it!

Aladdin exits, waving good-bye to her. Elsewhere the two Chinese Police enter ceremonially

Bamboo The Emperor and Empress!
Typhoo (*a very quick cheer*) Hooray!
Bamboo The Grand Vizier!
Typhoo Hooray!
Bamboo And his son, *Prince Pekoe.*
Typhoo Boo!

The Emperor, Empress, Princess and Pekoe enter with Attendants

When the arrogant Prince Pekoe hears this "boo" he points threateningly at Typhoo

Pekoe (*enraged*) Silence, idiot!
Typhoo Pardon, o Important One. (*He bows his head*)
Pekoe I should think so too.
Typhoo (*aside to the audience*) It's (*name of trade union leader or politician*)

Pekoe joins the group who are being organized by the Vizier

Vizier Your Majesties, Your Royal Highness, my dear son Prince Pekoe, if you will be seated.

They sit on a bench at the side of the stage

(*Announcing*) To celebrate the Princess's birthday we have the Conjuror from Cairo, the Illusionist from Egypt—the Great Abanazar!

All applaud. The Vizier stands by the wings

Two Arabian-style turbanned conjuror's Assistants enter and usher in the imposing and wicked Abanazar, who enters

Abanazar bows to the Royal Family and then turns to the audience, in the Arabian way—fingers touching his forehead

Abanazar (*loudly announcing to the audience*) Now for some mind-boggling magic! So on with the show! Hey presto! (*He pulls a bouquet of feathered flowers from his sleeve*) Let the magic of Ancient Egypt now begin!

Loud and grand oriental music is heard (4a), and continues softly under the whole of the Magic Show sequence. Each trick is accompanied by much percussion, drum rolls and cymbal clashes

Various Attendants in Ancient Egyptian headdress or Arabian turbans— not Chinese—enter, and one hands Abanazar a brightly coloured cardboard box

(*Displaying it to those on stage and to the audience*) Your Majesties and all others, I have of course nothing up my sleeve. Let me show you this Ancient Egyptian box and see—by the gods of the Pyramid—it is empty. (*He opens the lid and shows the box is empty*) If some kind person will look after it for me. Thank you, sir. Hold on to it tight. (*He hands it to the Vizier, who is by the wings*) Kindly put it behind your back.

The Vizier does so

KALAKAZOOOOM! (*He waves his arms*)

There is a flash in the footlights. At the other side of the stage a Girl screams

It's all right, my dear. Just a little Egyptian magic.

This incident takes attention from the Vizier. A stage-hand exchanges the empty box for an identical cardboard box, and this the Vizier now holds behind his back

And now sir, may I take the box from your safe keeping? I thank you. See, from this absolutely empty box I produce *the flag of Wan Lung Soo.* (*He hands the box to one of his Assistants to hold, and takes out a large flag which he opens out and hands to his Assistant. The Court applauds*)

An Assistant hands Abanazar a blackboard slate and a piece of chalk

And now if Her Royal Highness will take this small slate and chalk, and write down any number she wishes, I will tell her what the numbers are! (*He hands them to the Princess*)

Princess (*taking them*) Any numbers?

Abanazar Any numbers you wish.

The Princess turns to audience

Princess (*in a confidential stage whisper*) What numbers shall we choose?

The audience call out. She whispers back

Five? All right! (*She chalks "5" on the slate*) Two? Three? ... (*When she has written "52319" she holds the blackboard slate away from Abanazar*) Tell me, oh Great Magician, what is the number on the slate?

Abanazar Er—er—five—two—three—one—nine.

Applause from the Court. Another Assistant hands Abanazar a large coloured bottle

Ah yes! If her Majesty will be pleased to take this bottle—it is a Truth Drug.

Empress A truth drug! There is no such thing!

Abanazar When you have drunk this Egyptian elixir, you will be compelled to tell the truth, oh ruler of the world.

Empress (*taking the bottle condescendingly*) This is not possible. I drink this and then I am compelled to tell the truth?

Abanazar Yes!

Empress Huh ... (*She takes a drink from the bottle and splutters*) OH— that was paraffin!

Abanazar That's the truth!

All laugh. The Vizier puts out his hand

Vizier (*shouting*) Ah-so!

All stop laughing instantly

Abanazar And now may I present the Egyptian Illusion entitled "A boat swimming on the River Nile". Here you see the River Nile ...

Two of his Assistants hold out a blue cloth between them. Unnoticed, one of the Assistants takes from behind her back a stick on the end of which is a toy yacht. She holds up the yacht and bobs it up and down along the top of the blue cloth. Abanazar takes a toy revolver from another Assistant and fires a blank at the yacht. We hear from the offstage microphone "glug glug" noises, the yacht is lowered slowly from view as though sinking, the music plays "Rule Britannia", Abanazar and those near him salute. The Chinese Court applauds. An Egyptian Assistant steps forward and hands to Abanazar a large envelope. Bowing, he gives it to the Princess

Your Highness.

Princess Oh! Oh I can't *do* anything you know. I'm a Princess!

Abanazar Most beautiful flower of the Universe, do you know what is in that envelope you hold?

Princess No.

Abanazar (*triumphantly*) Absolutely *correct*. (*With a flourish he whips out a large card with "NO" written on it from envelope*) Applause and cheers for her Highness! (*He sees the magic plant*) Ah! Now let me offer you a bouquet of flowers, your Highness! (*He crosses to the magic plant*)

Audience Wishee!

Wishee pops up from some unlikely place and runs in

Wishee Thanks, kids! (*He points to Abanazar*) You—Evil Canevil—put that plant down!

Abanazar (*surprised*) Pardon?

Wishee Granted!

Wishee runs off again and exits

Abanazar (*as though Wishee is all part of the act*) Now he's here—now he's not!

An Assistant hands Abanazar a second large envelope and he gestures to Pekoe

Prince Pekoe!

Pekoe Yes Magician?

Abanazar (*giving him the envelope*) I want you to think of a famous person and I will produce a photograph that looks exactly like that person. Tell me the name of the person of your choice?

Pekoe (*to the real audience*) Who shall we choose? Who? (*Any person that the audience suggests will do, say it is George Best*) George Best!

Abanazar I take out the photograph! Voila!

Drum roll as Abanazar takes out large photo of a baby from the envelope

There is a photo of George Best—*when a baby*. I thank you!

Prince Pekoe laughs and all on stage applaud

And now, the Miracle of the Pharoahs. Behold, The Floating Woman!

Two Assistants bring on a bench. A girl Assistant lies down on the bench, Abanazar takes a large cloth from an Assistant and drapes it over the girl. Unseen, he also gives her prop sticks with shoes on the ends similar to the girl's shoes. Abanazar moves away and makes mysterious passes at the girl lying under the cloth

Listen to the magic spell
That Abanazar declaims!
Margaret Thatcher! David Owen! (*Using topical names*)
And other terrible names!

The girl appears to levitate. She gradually sits up, her feet now on the ground, and she holds out in front of her the prop sticks so that her "feet" appear to be in mid-air and her body also.

She slowly exits. All gasp in great amazement and then applaud

And now for my last fantastic illusion brought to you all the way from Egypt! I present The Cabinet of Cleopatra!

Two assistants push on an oriental style wardrobe cabinet with curtain at the front and curtain at the back. It is placed near the wings

A Girl enters seductively

(*Presenting her*) Here is Zaida, my beautiful Egyptian assistant, who will now enter the cabinet.

Emperor (*seeing the beautiful girl and wriggling*) Ooooo, I say!

The Girl sways close to the Emperor then moves on to the cabinet, enters and closes the curtain

Abanazar May I have an assistant from the audience for this trick?

Emperor (*with great enthusiasm*) Yes!

Empress (*with great fury*) No!

Abanazar Stand up, Majesty!

Empress Sit *down*, Majesty! Stop making a fool of yourself.

Emperor (*scared of her*) I am Emperor. My will is law—well it is sometimes. (*He toddles over to the cabinet and waits, rubbing his hands together in anticipation*)

Abanazar I will now reveal why it is called Cleopatra's Cabinet! Behold— Cleopatra herself!

There is a drum roll and a cymbal crash

Widow Twankey steps out in a huge turban, or vaguely dressed as Cleopatra

Twankey Hello, cheeky! Come and have a date behind the palms!

Emperor Oh, calamity!

Confusion. Everyone shouts to each other, the enraged Empress stands up

Empress This is outrageous! Everyone is dismissed! You Vizier and you Prince Pekoe, order the magician to tidy up and leave this place at once! Chopsuey, come here!

The Emperor, a much disappointed man, examines the cabinet

The Empress grabs the Emperor by the ear and exits with him. All the others exit also, talking in shocked tones, except Abanazar, the Vizier and Prince Pekoe

Vizier You, you untalented son of an Egyptian camel driver, tidy up your magical objects!

Obsequiously, Abanazar starts to tidy up

Pekoe Huh! You'll never find success in China, will he father?

If the optional prologue is not used, ignore this line and continue

---

Vizier Find success in China? *Never.* (*Conspiratorially leading Pekoe* *downstage*) My boy, I wish to talk urgently with you. It's about your future.

Pekoe (*scheming evilly*) My future?

Vizier Yes, you—*and the Princess.*

Pekoe The Princess! Aha!

They scheme together in mime. Abanazar turns to the audience

Abanazar (*aside to the audience*) Those two fools don't know my secret! I'm not in China to find success. I'M IN CHINA TO FIND THE MAGIC LAMP! The only thing is, where is it? Must I search the whole of China for the Magic Lamp?

Abanazar returns to tidying up various magic tricks, the cabinet etc, while away from him the other two continue to scheme

Vizier Soon you will be *married* to the Princess, my boy!

Pekoe But she doesn't care about me! She doesn't even look at me!

Vizier (*cunningly*) She will—*soon.*

Pekoe What do you mean, Father?

Vizier You know the Cave of a Thousand Jewels near Pekin?

Pekoe The cave in the mountains? Yes!

Abanazar starts to listen

Vizier You know that no-one can unlock it's door?

Pekoe Yes!

Vizier I have discovered the secret from this old book. (*He takes a book from his pocket*) See. "Here is the secret of the cave near Pekin".

Pekoe (*much excited*) Well what is the secret? *What is it?*

Vizier You just say "God is Good".

Abanazar is still listening and, like the other two, is mystified

Pekoe I *know* God is Good. What's that got to do with it?

Vizier (*frustrated*) I don't know! I stood outside the cave yesterday and I called out "God is Good" but nothing happened.

Pekoe (*frustrated*) Curses! If I could get the jewels in there, *I could get the Princess.*

The Vizier looks round each way and particularly checks that Abanazar is not listening. Abanazar pretends he is not

Vizier Not the jewels in there, THE LAMP in there.

Pekoe (*curious*) The Lamp?

Vizier (*declaiming*) He who holds the Lamp, holds THE WORLD in his sway!

Pekoe (*excitedly*) The Magic Lamp! I've heard of it! (*In more frustration*) But father, *how can we get into the cave?*

Vizier (*beside himself with frustration*) I don't know! All I know is the secret words "God is Good". Let's go home and think it out. (*Puzzled and desperate*) "God is Good—God is Good . . ."

Pekoe "God is Good—God is Good . . ."

The mystified and much frustrated Vizier and Pekoe exit

Abanazar laughs with triumph

Abanazar Ha ha ha ha ha! *So!* The Magic Lamp is hidden in a cave near Pekin! I'm on the right track! But what does the secret mean? "God is Good"? (*He laughs*) Why, it doesn't mean anything more in Egyptian! "Allah—eh—din." "Allah—eh—din." (*To the audience*) What's the matter? You seem to know something! Is "Allah—eh—din" a town near Pekin?

Audience No!

Abanazar Then where is this town called "Allah—eh—din"? Wait a minute! *Is* it a town? (*He realizes*) Is it a *person*?

Audience Yes!

Abanazar Boy or girl?

Audience Boy!

Abanazar Thank you! You've made my old heart gladden!
　　　　So now to find the boy Aladdin!
　　　　And now to tell you my evil ambition:
　　　　From the whole of the world I demand Submission!
　　　　You've heard of Darth Vader? Well I'm worse!
　　　　I want to rule the Universe!

He sneers at the audience

　　　　And I *shall* rule the Universe, you ignorant shower
　　　　Once I have Aladdin within my power!
　　　　Ha ha ha ha ha ha!

Waving his fist, Abanazar exits to boos. From the other side, Aladdin enters with a bag of laundry. The Princess enters also

---

Princess Aladdin! What are you doing here?

Aladdin I've come with the palace laundry! Nothing wrong in that, is there?

Princess You've really come to see me, haven't you?

Aladdip (*laughing*) Of course! (*He chucks the laundry upstage*) Who cares about laundry when there's a pretty Princess to be with! (*He takes her hand*) I can't keep away.

They gaze at each other

The two Police enter upstage, casually as though on the beat. Suddenly they see the lovers, jump in the air and blow their whistles

Bamboo It's Aladdin!

Typhoo It's the Princess!

Bamboo Call the police! Call the police!

Typhoo (*hitting him*) We're the police, you twit!

Princess It's the police!

Aladdin (*pointing off*) And look—the Emperor and Empress!

Princess My mother and father—run Aladdin—if you're caught you'll lose your head!
Aladdin (*grinning*) I've lost it already!
Princess Run!
Aladdin Run from you? You must be joking! (*He stays there, gazing at her*)

The Emperor, Empress, Vizier, Pekoe, the Executioner with his axe, and all the Citizens enter. The Executioner wears the black domino mask and looks frightening, threatening with his axe or scimitar

Emperor (*to Aladdin, pointing his finger*) You are a naughty little boy.
Empress (*enraged*) Oh my ancestors! He looked at the Princess! Off with his head!

The two Police grab Aladdin

Princess No! Save him! Mother, Father, I plead with you!
Empress Nonsense! (*She strides away down to the magic tree*) What's this?
Audience Wishee!

Wishee runs on

Wishee Thanks, kids!
Vizier (*with relish*) You're in time for the execution!
Wishee Stop! Stop! This can't go on!
Vizier (*thunderously*) *What* can't go on!
Wishee This—it's too small. (*He holds up a very small vest*)

Widow Twankey runs on and appeals to the Empress

Twankey Spare him! Spare him! Don't chop his head off.
Empress (*booming*) Why not?
Twankey He'll have nowhere to put his hat!
Emperor Perhaps we should spare him, dear.
Empress I'm giving the orders.
Twankey Oh good, I'll have a Guinness.
Empress (*to the Executioner*) Off with his head!

Drum rolls start. The Executioner steps forward. The Police force the now scared Aladdin to the ground

Vizier Citizens of Pekin! Time for the execution!

All stand in a tableau. The Executioner holds the axe above Aladdin's head. It is a serious moment. The drum rolls

Abanazar enters downstage and sees what is happening

Abanazar (*rubbing his hands together*) A juicy execution—just what I like.
Vizier What is your name, you foolish boy?
Aladdin Aladdin Twankey.
Abanazar (*with a huge reaction*) ALADDIN! (*To the audience*) Did I hear right, is that boy there Aladdin?
Audience Yes!

Abanazar So *that's* Aladdin. He mustn't die!
        'Cos I will need him bye and bye!
Twankey (*with her hands clasped in prayer*) Oh, your Maj, oh, your Imperial Leather, can I axe you something? Don't axe him.
Vizier Silence, woman. (*To the Executioner*) On the count of three, kill him. ONE!
All (*in a gasp of horror*) Ah!
Vizier TWO!
All (*another gasp*) Ah!

Abanazar runs c *and waves his arms at the Executioner*

Abanazar Evil spirits of the night
        Save Aladdin from his plight!
        ZABUNDA! ZABUNDA! ZABUNDA!

The Executioner shakes like a jelly, his St Vitus dance continues

Executioner Yes—you—er—war—wah—er—er . . .

All gaze flabbergasted at the Executioner. Abanazar lifts the petrified Aladdin to his feet

Aladdin Oh, thank you for saving me!

Now everyone starts to get the shakes to the continuing percussion

Abanazar ABRACADABRA ABRACADEE
        TURN INTO A STATUE FOR ME!

At once all stand still. Their "shakes" have got them into extraordinary positions for the "frozen statue" spell and they are more or less in a straight row. The Emperor is posed like a monkey. Abanazar goes to Twankey and Wishee and clicks fingers in front of their faces, so that they "come to"

Twankey (*amazed*) It's Madame Tussauds!
Wishee It's the meeting of the County Council (local reference)!
Abanazar Come, Aladdin, I've set you free!
        Come, my boy, come away with me!

Abanazar takes Aladdin's hand and they both exit

Twankey (*to the audience*) Shall we have a bit of fun?
Audience Yes!
Wishee Which first?
Audience The Empress!
Wishee (*to the Empress*) All right, Hilda Ogden, you stupid old geezer! (*He places her in some comical position. To the Vizier*) And you take that! (*He calls the Vizier some current villain's name, and kicks his bottom, then reacts and hops about*) Ow!
Twankey (*to the Emperor, who is still posed like a monkey*) It's Tarzan of the Apes. I'll let you get your own back on your missus! (*She holds the Emperor's fingers to his nose as though "thumbing" the Empress*)

Chattering animatedly to the audience, Twankey and Wishee arrange the

more or less straight row of people, probably in the following order, along the
footlights, from left to right: Vizier (with his bottom sticking out as he is bent
over), Strong Pong (with scimitar in the direction of the Vizier) Empress,
Emperor, Bamboo, and Typhoo who holds out his right arm like a stiff lever.

Now Twankey makes a great thing of pushing down Typhoo's right arm, and
then Typhoo's left arm shoots out and hits Bamboo, who kicks the Emperor,
and the Emperor at once hits the Empress with his left arm, she hits Strong
Pong who then suddenly pushes forward the scimitar he is holding and thus
"gooses" the Vizier who lets out a very loud "OW". On the very loud "OW"!
shout, Wishee and Twankey laugh and applaud and INSTANT BLACKOUT

Scene 2

RADIO RICK SHAW HIRE SERVICES, LTD

Tabs, or a front cloth of a Chinese Street, the main building being a radio
taxi shop front with various banners and Chinese notices on it

Aladdin and Abanazar enter

Aladdin By gum, how did you save my life?
Abanazar (*expansively*) My boy, I'm an Egyptian Magician! My magic
will help you any time, any time at all!

Twankey and Wishee enter. Twankey carries a large handbag or holdall

Twankey Oh, hark—he's full of Eastern Promise!
Abanazar (*indignantly*) Are you critizing me? *I* can walk down the Street
of a Thousand Chopsticks and turn into an elephant.
Wishee I can walk down—(*Local street*)—and turn into a chemist's.
Aladdin (*shaking hands with him*) Well, I must thank you, Mr—er—er . . .
Abanazar (*expansively*) Meet your Uncle Abanazar!
Aladdin Uncle who?
Abanazar Not Uncle who or Doctor Who, but ABANAZAR!
Twankey Thanks, but I'm not hungry.
Abanazar What?
Twankey You said "'Ave a banana".
Abanazar I said—(*Slowly*)—Abanazar . . .
Twankey What a funny name. (*To the other two*) He says his name is
Abbey National.
Abanazar (*tersely*) Abanazar.
Wishee Abernana? You're a right nana with a name like that. I should
change it!
Abanazar (*fed up*) ABANAZAR! ABANAZAR!
Twankey ⎫
Aladdin ⎬ All fall down! ⎰ (*Speaking*
Wishee ⎭   ⎱ *together*)
Twankey Well, Mr Ebenezer, I think you're wonderful.
Aladdin Not Mr Ebenezer, Mother. He did tell you. His name is
Abracadabra.

Abanazar (*hysterically stamping feet and shouting at him*) I—am—Aba—na—zar!
Wishee (*also hysterically stamping feet and shouting back*) There's—no—need—to—shout!

A girl with a permanent grin enters wearing a uniform coat and cap with "RICKSHAW" on the band. Also gauntlet driving gloves. She bows perkily

Rick Shaw (*with a quick bow of her head*) Ah so! Plenty biggee noise! You wantee something?
Abanazar Is this the Radio Rickshaw Hire Service?
Rick Shaw (*with a quick head bow*) Ah so! I am Ladio Lickshaw.
Wishee (*waving to her*) Hello, Rick!
Rick Shaw Hello, Lishee!
Abanazar I want to hire a rickshaw from you.
Rick Shaw (*bowing her head*) Ah so!
Abanazar I want to go up into the mountains and take this boy Aladdin with me.
Rick Shaw (*bowing*) Ah so!
Twankey Oh, not to the Magic Cave! Oh help!

All laugh except Abanazar

Wishee (*to Rick Shaw*) Everyone's been up there, haven't they?
Rick Shaw (*nodding*) Ah so!
Wishee (*to Abanazar*) And I suppose you want to try and open the magic door!

All laugh except Abanazar

Aladdin (*to Abanazar*) Thank you for saving my life, Uncle, but I've got better things to do than go to that old cave! I'm off to see my Princess again!
Abanazar (*anxiously*) But I've discovered that *only Aladdin* can enter the cave!

All laugh again except Abanazar

Rick Shaw (*with a little bow to Aladdin*) Honollable Ladio Lickshaw at your service! I take you to honollable cave in honollable lickshaw!
Aladdin What? At the price rickshaws are now? (*He appeals to the audience*) From the station to Lewis's is two pound fifty—aren't I right? (*Whatever is a local expensive taxi fare joke*)

Aladdin starts to exit

Abanazar No! Come back, Aladdin! I *must* go to the cave!
Aladdin Well, I must go to the Princess—ta ta! Come on, Wishee!
Wishee Just a minute, I want to experiment. (*To Rick Shaw*) You—Little Noddy—you're stupid, you're barmy, and you've got the brain of a three-year-old nincompoop, now haven't you?

Rick Shaw (*apparently pleased, nodding*) Ah so!
Wishee You have? (*Overjoyed*) Then we were made for each other! Come on, we'll get some Chinese Take Away!

Wishee takes her hand or gives her a piggyback ride, and Aladdin, Wishee and Rick Shaw exit

Abanazar But Aladdin *must* take me to the cave! That boy will drive me crazy! You're all crackers!
Twankey Chinese crackers! (*She does a mad gesture*) Boom boom!
Abanazar I shan't be able to sleep thinking about that cave. All night there'll be a voice calling to me, "Come to the cave! Come to the cave!"
Twankey Oh, I think I might have something to help you sleep.
Abanazar What's that?
Twankey Being a magician it will interest you. (*Proudly*) It's a magic hat— there! (*Out of her large handbag/holdall she takes a fez of the kind that can be easily held and holds it up*)
Abanazar Where did you get that?
Twankey From the Turban District Council.
Abanazar But why will it help me sleep?
Twankey Put it on and you won't hear a sound.
Abanazar If I wear that thing I won't hear a sound?
Twankey That is correct.
Abanazar Don't be ridiculous, woman. (*To the audience*) This is a bit of hanky panky from Widow Twankey.
Twankey No it's not. When this hat is on your head you won't hear anything at all.
Abanazar Huh—prove it! (*He removes his own hat*)
Twankey Certainly I'll prove it. I'll prove it right now. Ready?
Abanazar (*very dubiously*) Ready.
Twankey (*with great emphasis as she embarks on her story*) *Well*, Abanazar dear, when I got this hat it was a lovely day so I went for a nice walk through Pekin when suddenly I . . . (*She clamps the hat on Abanazar's head and at once she becomes silent but continues her story in mime. Apparently she is describing some amazing and shocking incident. After a few seconds she lifts the hat from off Abanazar's head and at once speaks again*) Covered in bright red spots! Yes, it's *true*! There it was, right in the middle of (*Local place*) Street! Well I was *amazed*! I was *flabbergasted*, because I . . . (*She puts the hat on Abanazar and at once stops speaking but continues in mime with the extremely dramatic telling of the story. After a few seconds she removes the hat again and instead of her lips moving with no sound, she says at once*) So I said "You cheeky monkey!" and d'you know what happened then? He picked it up and he *threw* it at me! Well I was so angry I . . . (*She clamps the hat on his head, mimes with great agitation and after a few seconds removes the hat again and at once speaks indignantly*) Half-past eight! And believe me or believe me not, *she hadn't got one either!* (*Her story ended, she relaxes and says triumphantly*) There now, you never heard a word when you had the hat on, now did you?

Abanazar (*much impressed*) No I didn't! It's a magic hat all right! How much do you want for it?

Twankey Well, as you're a friend of mine—ten quid.

Abanazar gives her the money, collects the hat and puts it on

Abanazar This is great! Now I'll be able to sleep!

Twankey Yes you will—no more noise—no more worries—no more thinking about the magic cave—oh, you'll be so pleased you bought it— you'll never regret it . . .

Twankey has forgotten that Abanazar is wearing the hat, but he has not

Abanazar (*realizing and interrupting her*) Just a minute! I can hear every blooming word you're saying! This hat isn't magic at all! I want my money back!

Twankey I'm sorry, I can't give it back.

Abanazar I tell you, I want my money!

Twankey Well I tell you, you can't have it!

Abanazar I can have it and I will have it! (*He has an idea*) I know, I'll sell it to someone else! I'll dress it up a bit. I'll put this plant on it. (*He takes off the hat and goes to the magic plant at the stage corner*)

Audience Wishee!

Wishee runs on

Wishee Thanks, kids! (*To Abanazar*) What d'you want, Mutton Chops?

Abanazar (*acting out huge sympathy*) Oh dear, oh dear, oh dear. You *do* look tired.

Wishee How funny you should say that! 'Cos I am tired. I'm not getting enough sleep.

Abanazar Don't worry about it! What you need is this. (*Holding it up*) It's a magic hat. Any time you put this hat on, you won't hear a sound.

Twankey You'll sleep like a baby. In that hat you'll hear nothing at all!

Wishee (*to them both*) Now don't be daft.

Abanazar We're not being! It really works! Mind you, I want paying for it.

Wishee How much?

Abanazar Well as you're a friend of mine—twenty quid.

Wishee Twenty quid? All right, if it means I can get some sleep it's worth it.

Abanazar Good, you'll soon get the hat—(*to Twankey*)—and we'll soon get twenty quid.

Twankey (*pleased*) Twenty quid—smashing.

Wishee But how does it work?

Abanazar Oh Widow Twankey works it wonderfully!

Abanazar gives Twankey the hat and she embarks on the dramatic telling of her story

Twankey (*with emphasis*) Well, Wishee, it all happened like this. There was this very old man, he must have been well over ninety, and one day he . . . (*She puts the hat on Wishee's head, mimes for a few seconds and then takes the hat off Wishee*) But the notice clearly said "Nudist Camp". Anyway, he climbed over the fence and there he saw the most amazing sight. It was a . . . (*She puts the hat on Wishee, continues in dramatic mime, then removes the hat saying indignantly*) So he squeezed it and squeezed it and d'you know what happened? *The end lit up.* (*Triumphantly*) There now, isn't it a marvellous magic hat? (*She holds the hat up for him to admire, but keeps hold of it*)

Wishee (*greatly impressed*) I didn't hear a thing!

Abanazar And it's only twenty pounds!

Wishee That's what I want to ask you about. Twenty pounds is a lot of money. I'm still a bit suspicious.

Abanazar (*with huge innocence*) Suspicious? How could you say such a thing?

Wishee I want more proof before I buy the hat.

Abanazar All right. We'll *both* prove it's worth. We'll sing to you, and no matter what sounds we sing, you won't hear anything at all. (*To Twankey*) Right?

Twankey Right.

They stand together like a pair of Victorian duettists and sing the music hall song slowly, seriously and unaccompanied. Wishee is on Twankey's R, near her

Abanazar ⎫ (*Together*) ⎱ Where did you get that hat
Twankey ⎭   ⎰ Where did you get that tile . . .

Twankey reaches out and plonks the hat on Wishee's head, so she and Abanazar mime the third and fourth lines of the lyric. She then removes the hat and they both loudly sing

> I should like to have one
> Just the same as that . . .

Twankey again puts the hat on Wishee, so they do not sing the next two lines of lyric. She then removes the hat from Wishee's head and they both sing loudly the last line

> Where did you get that hat—yeah!

They repeat this chorus very quickly with the same tacets on the alternate sections of the lyric and Twankey does the same "hat off" business, and they end in "Big Time" style. Twankey and Abanazar bow and curtsy extravagantly. But Twankey has accidentally left the fez on Wishee's head. Wishee watches them both as they "acknowledge the applause"

(*To the audience, after song*) Thank you for your kind applause—it is good of you—God Bless—you're a wonderful audience, the best one we've had tonight—thank you from the bottom of my heart—thank you, thank you.

Wishee starts to exit, wearing the fez

Abanazar (*noticing*) Hey! If you want the hat, where's the money?

Wishee's face goes blank

Twankey He said, *where's the money?*

Wishee's face goes blanker

Abanazar⎱(*Speaking together*) ⎱THE MONEY!
Twankey⎰   ⎰

Wishee Sorry. (*He calls out*) I can't hear a thing with this hat on!

Wishee runs off, chased by the loudly protesting Twankey and Abanazar

Abanazar⎱ (*Speaking*) ⎱ You cheat! Where's our money! Come back!
Twankey⎰ *together*   ⎰

The three exit on one side to loud vaudeville music, as Aladdin enters from the other side

Aladdin I've just been back to the palace but I can't find the Princess. (*He looks off, then asks the audience*) Here, was that Uncle Abanazar with my mum and Wishee?

Audience Yes!

Aladdin Then as I can't find my Princess I *will* go with him to the cave! If we can open the door we can get the treasure and go fifty-fifty! Then I'll be so rich I'll be able to *marry my Princess*. I think Uncle Abanazar will be able to open the cave. You see, he has black magic—and I don't mean the chocolates. If you've got black magic you can do anything!

Aladdin sings to a fast tempo

SONG 5

As Aladdin sings, the Citizens of Pekin enter and sing with him

During this Production Number the tabs open or the front cloth rises on the next scene

SCENE 3

WIDOW TWANKEY'S LAUNDRY

It seems to be mainly made of bamboo. If possible there are several practical doors upstage but these are not essential. There are notices such as "Dly Cleaning" and "Blingee and Takee Back Same Day" and "Lomo Adds Blightness"

After the Production Number, Aladdin and the Citizens exit. As they go, Twankey and Wishee enter the other side. Both wear bright coloured plastic coats made to look Chinese in style

Twankey (*calling*) Ching Ching! Sing Lo!
Wishee (*calling*) So Long! Ping Pong!

Four of the Citizens enter

Citizens Yes, Mrs Twankey? What is it, Wishee?

Twankey Wishee and I would like you to help us with the laundry.
Wishee Help us with the dirty work!
Citizens We stay! We help! We bow! (*They bow*)
Tankey Then welcome to my lovely launderette!
Wishee (*organizing*) Everybody collect a tub!

*The four Citizens collect wash-tubs from upstage and stand in a downstage
line with them*

Twankey (*as they get ready*) Here's a bit of advice. Don't put your cat in
the washing-machine or you'll get a sock in the puss!

They all laugh

Wishee (*in a child-like voice, taking Twankey's hand*) Oh Mummy, why
are your hands so soft Mummy? Your hands are always so soft, why
are they so soft?
Twankey (*to the four Citizens*) I'm soft in the hands and he's soft in the
head. (*She holds up a big prop packet of Tide from one of the wash tubs*)
Wishee (*in a plummy voice, as though an interviewer in a commercial*) Excuse
me, madam, why do you always do your laundry in Tide?
Twankey Because it's too cold to do it out-tide. (*She turns to the four
helpers*) Now let me explain. Wishee has been very stupid. He's lost the
laundry list and we've got to remember whose laundry is whose. (*To the
First Citizen*) So what's in your tub?

*She takes pad and pencil from her apron pocket and First Citizen holds up
bright red underpants from out of the first tub*

Wishee (*looking at them*) Red pants—Arthur Scargill's!

*Twankey writes down the name. The Second Citizen holds up a large blue
pair of old-fashioned bloomers from the second tub*

Twankey (*seeing them*) Blue—*true* blue—Mrs Thatcher's!

*She writes it on her pad as the Third Citizen holds up a huge pair of under-
pants*

Wishee (*laughing*) The *liberal* candidate's! They're Cyril Smith's!
Twankey They're a politician's bloomer all right!

The Third Citizen turns them round and shows a hole in the back

Oh look, he's an MP and he's lost his seat!

*As Twankey notes the name on her pad the Fourth Citizen holds up a big
pair of coloured bloomers*

Wishee Those are Barbara Cartland's (*or topical name*)
Twankey Shouldn't they have lace round the bottom?
Wishee No, only round the legs.

*As Twankey notes the name, the First Citizen holds up a very small bra
indeed*

Twankey (*starting at it*) A bit small, isn't it? Has it shrunk in the wash? Oh I know, it's Olive Oyl's.

As she notes it, the Second Citizen holds up a very large bra

Wishee (*looking at it*) Great Scott what a lot—Barbara Windsor's.
Twankey Of course!

She notes it and the Third Citizen holds up a bright pink bra

Oh, that's the Shirley Williams bra.
Wishee The Shirley William's bra?
Twankey It makes mountains out of molehills.

As Twankey notes the name, so the Fourth Citizen holds up a dark blue bra

Wishee That belongs to Policewoman Plod. She wears it for night duty.
Twankey She wears it for night duty? How do you know?
Wishee Watch. (*Calling out*) Night Time, Please!

The Lights fade to a Black-out. The Fourth Citizen switches on a battery and two bulbs light up in the "correct" places. The Lights come up again and Twankey writes as the First Citizen holds up a bra with three "cups" instead of two

Twankey (*seeing it, and reacting*) Help! Two cups and one for the pot!
Wishee What a funny lady! Who is she?
Twankey Miss Er . . . (*She laughs*) Miss Stake if you ask me! Next!

The Second Citizen holds up another bra

Wishee That belongs to a BOAC pilot.
Twankey What are you talking about, a BOAC pilot!

Wishee takes the bra and puts it over his head like earmuffs, then hands it back. Twankey notes it, and the Third Citizen holds up a large bra

Oh I say, that's for a bouncing girl!
Wishee How d'you know?
Twankey I'll show you.

She collects the bra and throws it hard on to the floor. It has two tennis balls sewn into it, and bounces. The Fourth Citizen holds up a piece of tape or ribbon on which is one large cup

Good gracious!
Wishee It's Lou Beale's! (*Or any T.V. soap opera comedy lady*)
Twankey But what a funny bra!
Wishee (*taking if from the Citizen*) It isn't her bra, it's her hat. (*He puts it on his head like a bonnet*)

Twankey notes the name, and the First Citizen holds up a soccer shirt clearly showing the colours of some well known local team. Wishee encourages audience applause

Twankey Yes, we do the laundry for a great team!

The Second Citizen holds up a similar soccer shirt, but full of big holes

Wishee Those are the holes in the team's defence!

The Third Helper holds up a man's shirt with a crown on the flap

Twankey (*shocked*) A crown on the shirt tail! Oh, who could be so rude
to royalty.
Wishee Willie Hamilton.
Twankey Of course.

*She notes the name, as the Fourth Citizen holds up a dark blue shirt with
big stars on it*

Wishee All those stars! Oh I know—it's Patrick Moore's (Russell Grant's).

*Twankey writes as the First Citizen holds up a pair of "longjohns"—
Victorian combinations. The flap has cardboard sewn on it to make it clearly
a flap*

Twankey Larry Grayson's! (*To the Citizen*) And shut that door!

*The First Citizen closes the flap upwards. Twankey notes, and the Second
Citizen holds up a pair of old fashioned corsets with a big padlock*

Wishee Mrs Lighthouse! (*He takes them and "plays them" as though they
are a concertina and sings the ice cream commercial*) "Just one Cor-
netto ...

The Third Citizen holds up a pair of man's pants that also have a big padlock

Twankey Lord Longford's!

*The Fourth Citizen holds up a pair of bloomers with two large letters—"D"
and "D"—on them*

Wishee Donald Duck's.
Twankey D.D. doesn't stand for Donald Duck!
Wishee What does it stand for, then?
Twankey Droopy Drawers!

*Other possible props are some leopard skin pants (Rod Stewart), a very small
pair of pants (Ronnie Corbett) a very big pair (Ronnie Barker)—whatever is
topical.*

Wishee Right! That's that! Now we'll iron them all!
Twankey Oh Wishee, I can't be bothered.
Wishee Then who will do the ironing?
Twankey We'll take them down the street to Mister Wu.
The Citizens Mr Wu?

Music starts

Twankey Yes, when we don't feel like doing the laundry, we always go
and have a chat to Mr Wu! (*She sings*)

SONG 6

The four Citizens take washboards and thimbles from the cut-out washtubs, and accompany Twankey and Wishee as they sing and it becomes a Production Number

At the end the four Citizens exit with their four washtubs

Wishee (*after the song, casually*) I forgot to tell you. I put the Emperor's comms in to starch.
Twankey *You what?*
Wishee I put the Emperor's comms in to starch.

He points to the upstage table on which are a laundry basket, various plastic bowls, buckets and some soda syphons and goes to it

Twankey (*horrified*) What have you done?
Wishee This.

He holds up from the basket a white hardboard replica of the full-length combinations. Twankey lets out a cry of horror and runs up to the other end of the table

Twankey You naughty boy! Bring the table down here!

They take it downstage to the stage cloth then Wishee holds up the "coms"

He can't wear those like that! We must get the starch off somehow!
I know! (*She picks up the soda syphon*) This'll get rid of the starch.

She accidentally squirts the water at Wishee, instead of at the hardboard comms he is holding

Wishee Did you do that on purpose?
Twankey Do what on purpose?
Wishee (*collecting another syphon and squirting it at her*) That!
Twankey Certainly not. I meant to hit the comms like *that*—(*she squirts*) —but I accidentally hit you like *that*. (*She squirts*)
Wishee You didn't do it accidentally.
Twankey I did. Take that you rude boy. (*She squirts him*)
Wishee Well, you take *that*. (*He squirts her*)
Twankey Stop! Stop! We must get on with the washee, Wishee. Where's the liquid soap?
Wishee Here. Green soap for the first wash . . .
Twankey No, red soap for the first wash, yellow for the second.
Wishee No. *Green.*
Twankey All right, we'll mix them.

They start pouring one plastic bucket of slosh into another, then Twankey pours the red slosh into a large flat plastic basin, Wishee watching

Wishee That should be green.
Twankey Red.
Wishee Green.

Twankey *Red.* (*She slams her hand down into the shallow basin of slosh and slosh flies everywhere*)

Wishee I told you not to lose your temper.

Twankey Me, lose my temper? Take that you insolent boy! (*She flips slosh at his face*)

Wishee How dare you. Take that! (*He flips slosh at her face*)

Twankey I've never been so insulated. Take that. (*She flips a lot more slosh*)

Wishee The same to you with knobs on. (*He flips a lot more slosh*)

Twankey Right. This needs more preparation. (*To the audience*) Then he'll get it! (*She stirs another plastic bowl*)

Wishee I agree, it needs more preparation. (*To the audience*) Then she'll get it! (*He stirs another plastic bowl*)

They both stir "evilly"

> *The Vizier enters in a white costume, nylon, or other material easily washed or instantly wiped off*

Vizier Now you two, for the last time, *where is Aladdin?*

Twankey and Wishee do not see him, but pick up their respective bowls or basins to throw at each other

Wishee ⎫
Twankey ⎭ One—two . . . ⎬ (*Speaking together*)

Vizier (*coming down between them*) I don't think you heard me, I said, where is Al . . .

Wishee ⎫
Twankey ⎭ Three! ⎬ (*Speaking together*)

The contents of bowls are flung full face at the Vizier. His white costume is covered in red and green slosh. Loud vaudeville music. The Vizier shouts with fury

> *The Vizier chases Twankey and Wishee off, all three exit. So Shi, the handmaiden, creeps in and looks round*

So Shi (*calling*) Aladdin!

> *Aladdin enters from the other side. He wears a bright-coloured apron and a bright small hat*

Aladdin Oh hello, So Shi, come about the palace laundry?

So Shi No. I have come about the Princess.

Aladdin What about her? Is something wrong?

So Shi Nothing wrong! Princess here!

> *The Princess runs on*

Princess Aladdin! (*Anxiously*) The Police! They're after you!

Aladdin I know—they tried to cut my head off so they'll try again!

Princess (*still anxiously*) So Shi, I must talk with Aladdin—will you keep guard.

So Shi Of course, honourable Highness. (*She bows and starts to exit*)
Aladdin And if you see my Uncle Abanazar, grab him. He's very good at rescuing me!
So Shi It shall be done.

So Shi exits

Aladdin We're alone at last!
Princess But I'm so worried for you!
Aladdin Oh I'm right—I'm always getting into scrapes! (*Excitedly*) Next thing for me to do is to go with Abanazar to the magic cave, bring back some jewels, give them to your father—and then he'll just *have* to say you and I can get married!
Princess (*laughing*) You do have the most incredible ideas!
Aladdin Well, I'm ambitious!

They both laugh. During their dialogue, the Chinese Police have been entering stealthily with Prince Pekoe and the Vizier. Pekoe remains at one downstage corner, the Vizier goes to the other one

Pekoe (*pointing dramatically*) There's Aladdin!
Vizier Grab him, you fools!
Bamboo Yes, Vizier!
Typhoo Certainly, sir!
Pekoe Aladdin, you're trapped!
Vizier We've got you at last.

The Police grab Aladdin C, and blow whistles

The Emperor and Empress enter

Emperor Naughty, naughty, you shouldn't be doing that, you know.
Empress Out of my way, husband! I'm the strong one round here. (*To the Princess, pointing to Pekoe*) Daughter, *that* is the man you will marry. (*She points to Aladdin*) And *that* is the man to be decapitated.
Emperor Decapitated? Couldn't he just have his head cut off?
Aladdin (*breaking free*) I love your daughter. What is wrong in that?
Empress (*gasping*) Oh my Imperial Ancestors! Grab him!

Aladdin runs down R but the Vizier is there

Vizier (*putting his hand up*) Stand back!
Aladdin Help! (*He runs down L, but Pekoe is there*)
Pekoe (*putting his hand up*) Stand back!
Aladdin Help! (*Calling*) Uncle Abanazar, where are you? Save me!

Abanazar enters

Abanazar What's the matter my boy?
Aladdin The fuzz have got me!
Abanazar Don't despair, all will be well
   I raise my hands and make a spell!

Twankey enters in a big brightly coloured mob cap and overall. Thus both she and Aladdin are wearing bright-coloured clothes

Twankey Make a smell? What on earth for? (*She sees everyone*) Help!
Vizier (*shouting*) Police, you will capture Aladdin *and his mother.*

The Police grab Twankey and Aladdin C

Abanazar STOP!

All stand still, frozen. Abanazar addresses the audience, then Aladdin

    Once more Aladdin I've managed to save,
    So take me boy, to the magic cave!
Aladdin (*gratefully*) Oh yes Uncle—to the magic cave!

Abanazar casts a spell on all those on each side of him

Abanazar Spirits of darkness help me again,
    Let chaos and confusion reign!

Abanazar stays C, *waving his arms. Instant Strobe lighting.*
The Offenbach Can-Can music (6a) starts played ff, not prettily. All run about confusedly

  Aladdin and Widow Twankey exit

The Vizier, Pekoe and the Police point clearly to the direction in which they have gone

Police ⎫
Vizier ⎭ There they are! ⎬(*Speaking together*)

They start to exit towards where Aladdin and Twankey went

 From the opposite side a man enters dressed in duplicate bright mob cap and overall, as though Twankey (2) and a girl enters with bright hat and apron like Aladdin (2)

They tap the two Police and the Vizier on the shoulder, and this makes the Police turn round

Police Waaah!

 The Police and the Vizier chase Aladdin (2) and Twankey (2) off. The real Aladdin and Twankey enter from elsewhere, see the offstage Police, point to where they are and exit up C

The following Grimaldi routine can work well with several doors in the scenery. The chase is in and out of the doors. If no doors are possible, the exits each side of stage, and up C *are used. The music is very loud, with many shouts from the Vizier and blowings of whistles from the Police*

 Aladdin (2) and Twankey (2) re-enter, creeping on, followed by the Emperor and Empress ready to hit them. As they creep across the stage, Aladdin (3) and Twankey (3) enter and tap the Emperor and Empress on

shoulders. The royal couple turn, scream, and chase the third couple of Aladdin and Twankey and exit up C *or into some of the practical doors. Now the real Aladdin and Twankey run across the stage followed by the Vizier and Pekoe followed by yet two more "Aladdins and Twankeys" followed by the Police, followed by the second batch of "Aladdins and Twankeys" followed by the Emperor and Empress. Abanazar bellows out a laugh of triumph and exits. The Police blow their whistles*

All Where are they? Where's Aladdin? Which is Aladdin? That's Widow Twankey! No it isn't, yes it is! Who are you? Which is what?

The real Aladdin and Twankey have exited for the last time, and all the others look round at each other

Who are you? You aren't Twankey! You're not Aladdin! What's happening! This is disgraceful!

The music reaches the place in the Can-Can where the best known part of the tune occurs. As they are all in a line anyway, they put an arm round each others' shoulders and do high kicks in time, moving downstage like a Tiller Girl line up. Then all the line kneel on one knee at the coda of the tune to end the chase sequence

After this, dancing to the reprise with high kicks again, all exit except the Emperor, Empress, Vizier and the two Police

These five move downstage

Empress (*recovering*) What are we doing? You let Aladdin escape—didn't you?
Emperor I'm sorry, dear.
Empress And you police are so hopeless, I shall ignore you.
Vizier But, your Majesty, does that mean you won't come to the Pekin Police Ball?
Bamboo We've got the Police Choir!
Typhoo For your Majesty's entertainment!
Empress *Entertainment?*
Vizier The Imperial Police Choir might please your Imperial Majesty.
Empress The Imperial Police Choir is an Imperial shower.
Police (*saluting*) Yes, your Maj.
Empress The best place to rehearse a choir like that one is up in the mountains, where no one can hear.
Police (*both saluting*) Yes, your Maj.
Empress Then let's *go* into the mountains and rehearse! Do you agree, Chopsuey?
Emperor No, dear.
Empress WHAT?
Emperor (*jumping*) I mean yes, dear.

During the above dialogue the front tabs close or the front cloth drops

SCENE 4

A PATH IN THE MOUNTAINS NEAR PEKIN

Tabs or a frontcloth showing mysterious rocks and a strong-looking door to the cave which must be practical

Empress Now. Which shall we sing, Nellie Dean, Nellie Dean or Nellie Dean.
All Nellie Dean.
Empress If you insist. (*To the Vizier*) Chow Mien, Nellie Dean, you are the conductor.
Vizier Yes, your Majesty.

The five stand in a row and sing, unaccompanied, "Nellie Dean". Straightway it is clear that the Emperor is singing flat as a pancake—soon the Vizier holds up his hand and takes a pistol from his pocket

STOP! (*Sinisterly*) *Someone's a rotten singer.*
All Four (*in turn*) Well, it's not me—or me—or me—or me.
Vizier (*as a command*) So right turn, by the left, quick march!

Percussion and heavy dramatic music

All march off fast. We hear an offstage gunshot, all march back again—except Bamboo

The Vizier blows on the end of the barrel of his pistol. The four stand in line and sing a few bars of "Nellie Dean" and again the Emperor is flat

STOP! (*Sinisterly*) *Someone's a rotten singer.*

All three look at each other apprehensively

All Three (*in turn*) Well, it's not me—or me—or me.
Vizier So right turn, by the left, quick march!

Percussion heavy funeral music

All march off. At once we hear the gunshot, and all march back except Typhoo

The Vizier blows on the barrel of his revolver. The three stand in a row and sing a few bars of "Nellie Dean". The Emperor singing very flat

STOP! *Someone's a rotten singer*

Emperor⎱
Empress⎰ (*in turn*) Well, it isn't me—or me.
Vizier Right turn, by the left, quick march!

Percussion, heavy music

All exit. We hear a gunshot and only the Vizier and Emperor re-enter

The Vizier blows on the barrel of his revolver. The Vizier and the Emperor stand together, the Emperor smiling at the Vizier, but scared. They sing a few bars of "Nellie Dean"

STOP! *Someone's a rotten singer*

The Emperor looks round, very nervous

Emperor I wonder who it is? (*Scared*) Well, it isn't me.
Vizier (*scowling at him*) Right turn, by the left, quick march!

The percussion and sombre music

> *Both exit. We hear an offstage gunshot. The Emperor re-enters, standing by the wings at the opposite side to the Musical Director*

Emperor (*triumphantly*) Ha ha ha—Someone's a *rotten shot.*

The Musical Director stands up and a spot picks him out

Musical Director (*shouting out*) Yes, but I'm not!

The Musical Director fires a gun at the Emperor, whose trousers fall down revealing combinations. He yells. A loud vaudeville chord. Black-out

> *The Emperor exits quickly*

The Lights come up again immediately

> *Abanazar enters, impatiently beckoning to Aladdin*

Abanazar Come on boy, come on!

> *Aladdin trudges on with no enthusiasm, tired*

Aladdin (*looking round*) We've walked for miles, the cave must be somewhere here!
Abanazar *I'll* be the one who has to find it! You lazy scamp, you couldn't find it if you tried!
Aladdin It's here. (*He calmly points to the door*)
Abanazar What? (*Seeing it*) Aha! Splendid!
Aladdin What's splendid about it? We'll need a squad from Wimpey's to shift that.
Abanazar Nonsense, I'll move it by magic. Watch! (*He waves arms at it*) Zabunda! Zabunda! Zabunda!
Aladdin Nothing!
Abanazar Then—Abracadabra!!
Aladdin Not a sausage.
Abanazar In Egypt we have a story called Ali Baba and the Forty Thieves ... (*To the audience*) What was the pass word that Ali Baba used? Open—open ...
Audience Sesame!
Aladdin What?
Audience Sesame!
Aladdin Ah yes, that's it. *Zebedee.* I once had a dog called Zebedee and—have I got the wrong name?
Audience Sesame!
Abanazar Of course! Salome! Why didn't we think of that. Salome and her seven veils. (*He calls to rock*) Open, Salome!

Aladdin Don't be silly, Uncle, even I know that's wrong. (*He hears the audience*) Open, SESAME? Thanks very much!

Abanazar makes magic pass at the rock

Abanazar Abracadabra. Abracadee,
          Open! Open, Sesame!

A crashing sound effect plus a loud dramatic chord, and the rock moves back to reveal the entrance to cave

Aladdin Didn't he do well!

Abanazar Stop fooling, Aladdin. No time to waste. In you go!

Aladdin In I go? I should co-co!

Abanazar (*sarcastically*) Scared?

Aladdin (*defiantly*) Yes! I'm not going in there!

Abanazar My boy, I sympathise. And to stop your worries, let me give this Magic Ring which will protect you from harm. (*He takes it off*)

Aladdin (*scoffing*) Magic Ring? How do I know you're telling the truth?

Aladdin (*very solemnly*) I swear by the gods of the River Nile that what I say is true.

Aladdin (*believing him*) Right then ... (*taking it and putting it on his finger*) Still, it doesn't look much to me!

Abanazar (*angrily*) Stop complaining! I've given you the Magic Ring, so now it's your turn to help me!

Aladdin All right, Uncle, I'll get the lamp for you. (*He steps inside the cave*) I'm in! I'm in!

Abanazar (*rubbing hands with glee*) He's in! He's in!

Aladdin I'm out. I'm out. I didn't realize it's so dark in there.

Abanazar (*fed up*) He's out. He's out. But remember the jewels for your Princess!

Aladdin The jewels for my Princess! Oh, that's different. I'm in again! (*He steps in*)

Abanazar He's in again!

Aladdin I'm out again—because I'm not sure I trust you.

Abanazar (*with enormous innocence*) *Me*. You don't trust *me*?

Aladdin Frankly no. (*To the audience*) Shall I trust him?

Audience No!

Aladdin Shall I go into the cave?

Audience No—yes—no—yes ...

Abanazar Oh yes he should!

Audience Oh no he shouldn't!

Abanazar Oh yes he *shouldn't* should!

Audience (*confused*) On no he ...

Abanazar shouts over the audience

Abanazar Yes yes yes! Think of your Princess!

Aladdin (*taking a heroic stance*) I'll do it—for my Princess!

   Aladdin exits bravely into the cave

Abanazar's "charm" vanishes, he laughs evilly

Abanazar The moment Aladdin gives me that old lamp
                Yours truly will quickly and quietly decamp.
                He'll never again see the earth and the sky.
                For inside the cave he will shrivel and die!
                Ha ha ha ha ha ha!

*Black-out. Instantly, loud frightening music—which fades down to silence.
In the silence we hear drip-drip sound effects. The front cloth rises or the
tabs open to reveal darkness except for one light—a small bulb in the
scenery, or a glow if the lamp is on a rock. During this, Abanazar runs up to
the back of the stage.*

SCENE 5(a)

INSIDE THE GLOOMY CAVE

*A dismal interior. Upstage, low down so that the audience can see, is the
now open entrance to the cave, with a practical door, at the moment not
seen as it is slid back. This door can easily be set at the upstage corner—a
sliding panel in a cut out that represents cave rocks*

Aladdin is upstage and moves down as though he has just entered the cave

Abanazar appears at the entrance and peers in

*Continued empty cave effects are heard—a couple of groans and weird
noises also*

Aladdin (*gazing round fearfully*) What a spooky place! And so dark!
    Reminds me of—(*local discotheque*)
Abanazar The lamp boy, the lamp!
Aladdin (*calling*) All right, keep your hair on! (*Looking round*) The lamp
    —where can it be—ah! (*He picks it up, in great disappointment*) Surely
    he can't mean this tatty old thing?
Abanazar Yes I do. Give it me, boy, give it me!
Aladdin (*calling*) Coming! (*Casually*) Oh, Uncle, where are the jewels for
    my Princess?
Abanazar Somewhere there . . .
Aladdin Yes but *where?*
Abanazar I don't know, boy. *Just give me the lamp!*
Aladdin I won't if you shout at me.
Abanazar (*very sweetly*) Would you be so good as to pass me the lamp.
Aladdin No. *Because where are the jewels?*
Abanazar Behind that rock there!
Aladdin What rock, where?
Abanazar Give me the lamp!
Aladdin Give me the jewels!
Abanazar Lamp!
Aladdin Jewels! (*In realization*) There's something funny going on here.
    (*To the audience*) Shall I give him the lamp?
Audience No!

Aladdin (*much surprised*) You mean, keep this rusty bit of rubbish for myself?
Audience *YES.*
Aladdin (*shrugging*) Whatever you say. (*Calling*) Uncle, I've decided *I'll* have the lamp, and you can have the jewels.
Abanazar I'll give you one more chance. GIVE ME THE LAMP!
Aladdin No, no, no, a thousand times no!

Percussion plays under the following

Abanazar Fool! Your life is ended, listen to my curse—
 For now the magic door will roll back in reverse!
Aladdin No, Uncle, no!
Abanazar You will be trapped and bye and bye
 You'll faint from hunger and you'll die!
Aladdin I didn't mean it, Uncle, I was only teasing!
Abanazar May rats and lizards around you prowl
 May you grow a moustache like Enoch Powell!
Aladdin No!
Abanazar May the spirits of darkness around you cling
 May you sound like—(*topical pop group*)—when you sing!
Aladdin Please, no!
Abanazar May your legs start to shrink, may you stagger and stagger
 May your mouth grow and grow, till you look like Mick Jagger.
Aladdin No, not that! Please! Please!
Abanazar Abracadabra, Abracadee
 Shut now I say, shut Sesame!

Thunder effects, dramatic chords, as the upstage rock slides shut

 Abanazar is blocked from sight

We hear the dripping sound, and melancholy music

Aladdin (*in horror*) He's locked me in! That means I'll never see my Princess again! (*Desperately running up to the entrance*) Uncle! I didn't mean to be cheeky! I quite like you in a way! Please open the rock, Uncle, please! (*He moves downstage and grabs the lamp*) Here, I'll give you the lamp! I don't want it!

A spider comes down from the flies, near him

 AAAAAH! Spiders! I'm so frightened—this horrible place and it's so dark and damp and dismal! (*Realizing*) He's locked me in here to die. TO DIE! What shall I do? What shall I do? This freezing place . . . (*He shivers*) What shall I do?

This is to invite the audience to shout

Audience Rub the lamp!
Aladdin What?
Audience Rub the lamp!

Aladdin What good will that do? Rub the lamp? What for? (*He rubs it*)

Flash

The Genie appears

Aladdin does not see it

I know it's dirty but how will rubbing the lamp help me to . . . (*He sees the Genie*) AAAAH! Who are you?

Genie (*bowing*) I am the slave of the lamp! Your wish is my command Oh Master!

Aladdin (*scared stiff*) Me—your master?

Genie (*nodding*) You have but to ask, and anything can be done.

Aladdin Can you help—(*local football team*)—get into the league?

Genie Even that, oh master!

Aladdin You *must* be good. Then you can get me out of this horrible cave?

Genie At once! (*Waving his arms*) Allakazam!

Dramatic chord and thunder, as the stone rolls open again

Aladdin If you can do that, can you help me to marry my Princess?

Genie (*nodding*) I will make you the richest Prince in the world.

Aladdin (*thrilled*) Me—Prince Aladdin? What will Mum and Wishee Washee say? (*Drily*) Oh, but you're just talking! Abanazar said there were jewels here in the cave, but I ain't seen nothing yet!

The Genie moves c and holds up his arms

Genie My lord! It is my pleasure!
Of the lamp I am the slave!
Behold! The thousand treasures
Hidden in the magic cave!

Loud music. Transformation. A fanfare plays and the dismal backcloth is flown, or the dark rocks part

SCENE 5(b)

THE ALCOVE OF A THOUSAND JEWELS

This is in great contrast to the gloomy cave. There are jewels and vases and chests of money and a general effect of dazzling splendour in the big alcove

Aladdin is astonished. The Slave Girls carrying jewel caskets start to enter

Genie Come, oh master—to see the secrets of the cave!

Aladdin exits, ushered off by the Genie

The Genie either exits with him or remains to sing the number. If the various Slave Girls and perhaps a Principal Slave Girl sings the number, the Genie exits

SONG 7

*After the Production Number/Dance Routine, the Genie enters or, if still
on stage, ushers in Aladdin who is now dressed magnificently*

*Slow march tempo of Aladdin's main song (Song 2), and he moves to
some rocks in the cave on which he stands, posed, to declaim*

Aladdin I who was cold and tired and wan
Am now a Chinese Elton John!
From rags to riches—once I was a tramp
AND I OWE IT ALL TO ALADDIN'S LAMP!

*He holds the lamp on high, all the Jewel Dancers and Singers and Slave
Girls arrange themselves for the Tableau. They and Aladdin sing the few
final bars of the reprise of*

SONG 2 (reprise)

GRAND TABLEAU

Curtain

NOTE: *The final couplet is altered to whoever is a topical and flamboyant
pop star. "I who was poor and cold and bitter, am now a Chinese Gary
Glitter" etc., etc.*

ACT II

AT THE FLIED LICE INN, A CHINESE TAKE AWAY RESTAURANT

The wings are bamboo style with Chinese banners on them and a very large menu: "Bizniz Man's Lunch. Birds' Nest Soup, Squashed Spider Sponge and Custard, China Tea or Cocee Colee—Six Yen" hangs on the wall. On stage are a few chairs and tables. Upstage is a terrace with a Chinese style balustrade across the width of the stage. Behind the balustrade are the roof tops of Pekin and rising up from them is a hill

Chinese people at the tables are being served by Waitresses in kimonos, others are chatting together. The Princess stands c with her two Handmaidens, So Shi and Sing Hi. The Princess sings

SONG 8

This becomes a Production Number with everyone joining in the song with the Princess

Princess (*after the song*) I don't know why I'm singing because I'm so worried!

Sing Hi Worried, Your Highness?

Princess Yes, Sing Hi. Aladdin has gone to the cave in the mountains— he should have come back long ago!

So Shi Maybe he *is* back and has gone to the laundry?

Princess The laundry! Good idea So Shi—we'll go to the laundry! That way we can avoid meeting the police! (*Beckons to everyone*) Come on!

The Princess and her Handmaidens exit, followed by all. From the other side, the two Chinese Police enter, blowing whistles

Typhoo Hey! I think I saw the Princess, she should be locked up in the Palace!

Bamboo (*to the audience*) Was that the Princess there?

Audience No!

Typhoo If she's got out of the palace we'll be in trouble! You wouldn't like that, would you?

All Yes!

Police Bloomin' cheek!

Twankey enters in outrageous gear

Twankey What's all the noise about?

Bamboo Hey, we want to see you, you're going to accompany us.

Twankey Lovely! I play the piano, I play it by ear. I've tried to play it with my hands but . . .

Typhoo Accompany us *to the police station.*

Bamboo (*in comedy—sinister tones*) For a little defective work.

Twankey Oh yes, defective work! I love defectives! Here, this is for you. (*She takes huge prop lollipop from her shopping basket*) "Who loves ya, babe"?

Typhoo We want to ask you where Aladdin is 'cos he's wanted by the Emperor and Empress.

Bamboo We can see Aladdin's not here. (*As a comedy—sinister threat*) But *you're* here.

Twankey I'm not here I tell you. I'm not here.

Bamboo and Typhoo point to their heads, registering she is mad

Look, I'm not in Hong Kong, am I?

Police No.

Twankey I'm not in Soo-Chung, am I?

Police No.

Twankey Well, if I'm not in those two places I must be somewhere else, mustn't I?

Police Yes.

Twankey And if I'm somewhere else I can't be here!

The Police look at each other and take off their helmets in Laurel and Hardy style

Typhoo I don't understand Stanley.

Bamboo I don't understand Olly.

Police We've got to find Aladdin
　　　　We've got to find Aladdin
　　　　We've got to find Aladdin
　　　　Yeah!

On the "Yeah" the Police kick up their right legs and exit

Twankey (*to the audience*) I've got to find Aladdin as well. I'm worried. He's such a juvenile detergent. If only someone had news of him . . .

Abanazar enters as though mourning some terrible tragedy

Ah, the very person! Am I glad to see you! (*To the audience*) It's Ali Baaaa-baaa, the black sheep of the family. (*To him*) I was just wondering what's happened to Aladdin!

Abanazar (*clasping his hands to his chest dramatically*) Sad news, Widow Twankey.

Twankey Don't tell me—the train fares—(*postage stamps*)—have gone up again.

Abanazar Worse than that.

Twankey *Crossroads* is coming off?

Abanazar Aladdin.

Dramatic chord

Twankey My boy, what's happened to my boy?

Abanazar (*with much melodrama*) Widow Twankey, prepare yourself.

Widow Twankey straightens her frock, smoothes her eyebrows, and pushes up her teeth with her thumbs

Twankey Yes?

Abanazar We were trying to find the magic cave . . .

Twankey Yes?

Abanazar We couldn't find it.

Twankey Yes?

Abanazar I thought to myself, I know what we'll do. We'll climb every mountain, ford every stream, follow every rainbow . . .

Twankey If you don't shut up I'll scream. Tell me about my *son.*

Abanazar It was on one particular bit of pathway through the mountains where we met this wild animal. (*To the audience*) You saw it happen, didn't you?

Audience No!

Abanazar Aladdin fought the animal fiercely, he was very brave, but the animal got Aladdin with its front paws . . .

The audience reacts to the above

(*To the audience*) Are you interrupting me? Aladdin and the animal wrestled and then—they both fell from the path down into the ravine. Twenty thousand feet below.

He looks down at the imaginary place. Twankey follows his gaze and, carried away, tries to see her son down in the ravine

Twankey Did he hurt himself?

Abanazar He's dead. (*To the audience*) *Isn't he?*

Audience No.

Abanazar Isn't he?

Audience No!

Abanazar You tell her the truth and I'll turn you into frogs—then you'll be hopping mad!

Twankey (*pathetically, to the audience*) Tell me it isn't true! Oh, my son!

Abanazar Aladdin is dead. He fell in a ravine. It was a tragedy.

The richly dressed Aladdin enters upstage, holding the lamp

Even now I can hear him saying with his dying breath . . .

Aladdin Hello, folks!

Abanazar "Hello fo . . ." (*He reacts, turns round*) *No.*

Aladdin Yes!

Abanazar *Curses.*

Twankey Aladdin! (*Seeing Aladdin's costume*) And in Danny la Rue's cast-offs!

Aladdin That snivelling wretch tried to lock me up in a horrible cave!

Abanazar It's not true!

Aladdin It is true. You took me in. But *look* what I took out! (*He holds up the lamp*)

Abanazar (*snarling with frustration*) The lamp! And I thought I was ever-ready!

Twankey Aladdin, wherever did you get all those clothes? Have you a Chinese Barclay Card?

He hands her the lamp

Aladdin Mum, you're always on about the housework. Give it a rub.

Twankey Well, it is filthy, dear. What a funny looking thing! (*She blows on it and rubs it with her dress*)

Upstage and unseen, the Genie enters and stands by Twankey and Abanazar, with a green spotlight on him

Abanazar now notices the Genie and is petrified. He shakes all over

Abanazar Dud dud er du du er dud er dud dud der der der.

Twankey (*amused*) He's got the collywobbles! The jim-jams! (*She laughs merrily, then also sees the Genie*) AAAH! Its the Jolly Green Giant! (*She salaams on the floor to it*) Salaam, salaam, she said, grovelling on the floor, salaam, salaam.

Genie Worry not, oh woman of easy virtue, I bring you good news!

Twankey Oh, *false* salaam! (*She gets up again*)

Aladdin But where's Wishee? (*To the Genie*) Send my brother to me.

Genie Come forth, oh Wishee Washee, wherever you may be!

Wishee jumps into view from the top of a step ladder hidden in the wings. He wears a nightshirt and nightcap and carries a trick candle. He does not see the Genie

Wishee (*a bit dazed*) Oh hello, Aladdin—I was just going to bed . . . (*He sees the Genie*) AAAAH!

The trick candle bends over at the sight of the Genie

Wishee Why are you dressed up like Jimmy Saville? And look—The genie with the light brown ale! (*Perhaps he sings this*)

Genie I wish to present to you my master, the Prince of Pekin.

Wishee (*to Twankey, with spitting effect*) The Pppprince of Pppppekin?

Twankey (*wiping her face*) Yes the Pppppprince of Ppppekin.

Wishee (*wiping his face*) Oh, I'd like to meet him, where is he?

Aladdin (*posing and making a fanfare sound*) Tarrarrr!

Twankey ⎱ YOU? ⎱ (*Speaking together*)
Wishee ⎰   ⎰

Wishee, Twankey and the Genie group around Aladdin, admiring his clothes, Abanazar creeps away, turns to the audience and speaks viciously

Abanazar I *hate* Aladdin, and this day he will rue
              Yes, I hate Aladdin—and what's more I hate you!

Abanazar starts to exit, to boos. The Twankey group sees him

Aladdin ⎫ Catch him! Bash him on the boko! Slap ⎫ (*Speaking*
Twankey ⎬ him in the chops! (*etc.*)   ⎬ *together*)
Wishee ⎭   ⎭

Loud chase music. The House Lights come up. Aladdin and Twankey and Wishee chase Abanazar into the audience where he tries to hide behind some children—who no doubt hit him—so he runs up on the stage again and Twankey grabs a "red-hot" poker from the wings, and moves near him

Abanazar (*with great dignity*) How did Aladdin escape? Someday I'll get to the bottom of this.

Twankey So will I! (*She "gooses" him with the red-hot poker*)

Abanazar AAAAH! (*He runs off, clutching his bottom*) You've not heard the last of me!

Abanazar exits

Aladdin That's got rid of him! Wishee, Mother, we're rich!

Twankey You can't fool yer old mother with them things—you've stolen that gear from—(*local man's shop*)—window.

Aladdin Mum, I never! Genie, show them some of my wealth!

Genie (*bowing*) You command and I obey! (*He claps his hands*)

To a few bars of oriental music a Slave Girl enters in the cave costume, carrying jewels from the cave scene. She put them down and exits

Twankey (*to the Genie*) Well, strike me pink!

The Genie thinks it is a command and waves his arms. Black-out, except for a pink spot on Twankey

(*To the audience*) Girls! I'm having one of my hot flushes!

Widow Twankey exits, fanning her face with her hands

Aladdin (*to Wishee*) And *you* will wallow in riches.

Wishee I what?

Aladdin You will wallow in riches.

Wishee I thought you said I'd swallow my breeches! I'm not quite with it tonight. I feel like rushing into Woolworths and shouting out Marks and Spencer!

Aladdin Show my *brother* how rich he is!

The Genie makes a magic pass at Wishee. There is a flash in the footlights, and Wishee is revealed in some gaudy pop costume

Wishee Coo— I look like (*topical pop star*)—fabulous! (*In an exaggerated American accent*) Hello, everybody! (*He does a couple of mad dance steps as he is now a contemporary pop star lookalike. He sings a few unaccompanied bars of a topical pop song*)

Aladdin (*pointing off*) But poor old Mum's not so fabulous, is she?

They both look off sadly

Wishee It's a shame. Look at the old girl, doing the laundry again.

Aladdin (*having an idea*) To please her, why don't I make her the most glamorous woman in China?

Wishee Not all the magic in the world could do that.
Aladdin Let's see. (*To the Genie*) Make my mother the most glamorous woman in China.
Genie You command and I obey!

The Genie makes a magic pass towards the wings. We hear razzy music Twankey enters in glittering finery, an exaggerated costume. Aladdin, Wishee and even the Genie are so impressed that they sing

SONG 9

Twankey (*after the song*) Isn't it lovely, now I need a boy friend to go with it. (*She strokes her dress*)
Aladdin How about—(*topical sports star*)
Wishee Oh, it's all happening! The glamour, the madness! Genie, take me to where the bright lights are!
Aladdin Where's that?
Wishee The—(*local*)—Electricity Showroom!

Wishee exits

Aladdin Now, Mum, I must take courage. (*He gulps at his own cheek*) Genie, bring me here the Emperor of China himself!

The Genie exits with a bow

There is a flash in the footlights

The Emperor and Empress run on at full speed. They stop suddenly c, *and are much bewildered*

Emperor (*looking round, scared*) Oh my ancestors, what's happening?
Twankey Hello, handsome!

The Empress is outraged at this

Empress (*gasping*) I know you—you work at the Chinese laundry!
Twankey That's me. I'm proud to say I'm the best scrubber in China.
Empress Oh! I am the Empress, aren't you going to address me correctly?
Twankey Certainly. Forty-two, Churchill Avenue—(*local place*).

Twankey exits

Aladdin bursts out laughing

Aladdin Oh, Mum!
Empress (*Seeing him*) You! It's you! You looked at my daughter—off with his head! Where are my Guards?
Aladdin Oh, don't bother with all that guff any more!
Emperor (*flabbergasted*) Dear boy, do you know who you're speaking to?
Aladdin Yes, my future mother-in-law.
Empress WHAT? Do you know who is the greatest person in the world?
Aladdin Yes. Me. (*Confidentially, man to man*) And I happen to know something about your financial position. The Royal Mint has a hole in it.

Emperor Oh! (*He giggles*) How did you know? Isn't he clever!

Aladdin (*cheerfully*) That's why you really can't say "No" when I ask for your daughter's hand in marriage!

Empress WHAT?

Aladdin I want us to be friends. I want to call you my old man.

Empress (*with outraged dignity*) He is the Emperor, head of the oldest family in China!

Aladdin All right then, I'll call you my old mandarin. (*Pleasantly*) Your Majesties, the reason I'm no longer afraid of you is that I have powerful magic. (*He pats the lamp worn round his neck*)

Empress Huh. Prove it.

Aladdin rubs the lamp

The Genie enters

Emperor ⎫ AAAAH! ⎫ (*Together*)
Empress ⎭   ⎭

Terrified, the Empress half faints, and the Emperor catches her

Aladdin I also love your daughter, and she loves me.

Empress Huh. Prove it.

Aladdin Bring the Princess here at once.

Genie You command and I obey. (*He waves his arms magically*)

The Genie exits

Flash in the footlights

The Princess runs on, then stops bewildered

Princess (*seeing Aladdin*) Aladdin—dearest—you're safe!

She rushes to him, they embrace, and over her shoulder the Princess sees the furious Empress

Oh, hello Mumsy!

The Emperor is convulsed

Empress Impertinent child!

Aladdin Princess, I am the richest man in the world.

Empress Huh. Prove it.

Aladdin (*to the Genie*) Yes—prove it!

Genie You command and I obey. (*He claps his hands towards the wings*)

Aladdin Those glittering H. Samuels rings
       Are just a joke when you see these things!

He gestures to the wings

The Genie ushers on two Slave Girls from the cave, to music (9a). They carry jewels from the cave scene—or, preferably, a simple "cut-out" of a barrel with "OIL" on it in large letters

The Emperor winks at the Girls and ogles them, but the Empress is flabber-gasted at what she sees

Empress Oh my ancestors! (*She tremblingly plays with the jewels—if oil barrel is brought on these will be the jewels brought on earlier*)

Princess (*aside to Aladdin*) Looks like the right time to ask Father.

Aladdin (*nodding*) Your Most Imperial Majesty, Ruler of the Empire of all China, may I have the honour of your daughter's hand in marriage?

Emperor Of course, my lad. By gum, we'll have the reception at—(*local place*)

The Empress has hardly heard, she is so transfixed by the jewels

Empress Yes, yes, yes, of course, what did you say your name was?

Aladdin Prince Aladdin.

Empress Aladdin—I know that name—can't place it ... (*She still concentrates on the jewels*)

Princess We must get the invitation cards printed!

Aladdin That's right! You mean something like this. (*Announcing grandly*) "Prince Aladdin of Pekin invites you to the wedding ceremony. It will be held in his magic palace built as a wedding present for his Princess!"

The Princess is delighted. Aladdin turns to the Genie

Have you got that Genie? Did you hear what I say? Build me a magic palace ...

Genie You command and I obey! (*He waves hands at the hill*)

Fanfare

All exit stylistically except the Genie

Percussion sounds. From behind the cut out ground row, where the bare hill is, we now see the pagoda-like palace appear, as though rising up out of the hill

And now while Widow Twankey is shedding
Tears of joy at Aladdin's wedding
I must prepare the aftermath
That is, the *wedding photograph.*

The Genie ushers Madam Flash Bang on. She is the Chinese Royal Photographer and she enters in a dark kimono and a top hat or bowler hat, with a camera on a tripod

Madam Flash Bang The Chinese People will want to see
Photographs plinted at half past flee
Of Loyal Wedding and interviews
On flont page of Pekin Evening News!
Ah so! (*She curtsies*)

Music starts

All the cast except Abanazar and Wishee enter chatting, and quickly arrange themselves in various chairs for the photograph group. The

Chinese Police organize. Twankey and the Empress wear big wedding style hats and those behind try and peep round. Pekoe chats with the Vizier

Madam Flash Bang meanwhile fussily runs up to arrange the group, then back to peep at it through the camera. She does not think the grouping is quite right, looks round for inspiration, sees the magic flower and goes to collect it

Audience Wishee!

Wishee enters in some comedy wedding costume such as a Chinese hat with pigtails and a huge daisy buttonhole

Wishee Thanks, kids! (*To Madam Flash Bang*) Naughty lady!

Wishee sees So Shi and goes to chat to her, while Madam Flash Bang finally manages to arrange everyone and returns to the camera

Madam Flash Bang Watchee Birdee!
Emperor (*looking up at the sky*) Where?
Empress (*hitting him*) Chopsuey, control yourself!
Madam Flash Bang Say cheese!
All Cheese!
Madame Flash Bang (*nodding*) Yang Tang Flash Bang. (*She clicks the camera*)

Wishee steps forward and sings first line of the song to the audience. Then each of the principals have a few lines each

SONG 10

Production Number and as they sing the Royal photographer is taking the group's photograph.

After the number, all except Aladdin and the Princess exit slowly, chatting

Aladdin and the Princess move downstage

Aladdin I'll go and see that the rickshaws are ready to take us on our honeymoon.
Princess And I'll check the luggage—my wedding trousseau!
Aladdin See you in a minute!

Aladdin exits, as So Shi and Sing Hi enter with an oriental trunk or chest

Princess Thank you So Shi, and you Sing Hi. Is this part of the luggage for the honeymoon?
Handmaidens Yes, Highness.
Princess I'd better see I've got everything.

So Shi lifts the lid, and the Princess rummages

Morning dress, afternoon dress, tea-gown, evening dress, sixty-eight pairs of shoes . . . Oh! Whatever's this old lamp packed for?

The Handmaidens do not know, so she holds up the lamp

Euuuurrrcch—it's so dirty! It'll mark all my lovely new dresses!
Abanazar (*off*) New lamps for old—new lamps for old . . .
So Shi Listen! It's an old pedlar calling his wares!

> *Abanazar enters disguised as a pedlar, with cowl over his head and wearing a tattered cloak. He carries a wooden rack with many lamps dangling from it, pedlar-style*

Abanazar New lamps for old! New lamps for old!
Princess New lamps for old? That seems a strange way to do business.
Abanazar (*in Fagin-style Jewish cockney*) I have my reasons, my dear.
Princess (*laughing*) They must be very strange reasons.
Abanazar They are my dear, they are indeed. New lamps for old! (*To the audience, impatiently*) She's beginning to get on my wick.
Princess Well, it's useful to have a lamp, but I want a clean one to take with me.
Abanazar (*holding one out*) Then here, my dear.
Princess That's fine! Why ever does Aladdin want a dirty old thing like this? (*To the Slave Girls, uncertain*) Shall I give it to the nice old pedlar?
Girls Yes, Princess.
Princess (*still uncertain, asking the audience*) Shall I?
Audience NO!
Princess (*jumping*) Oh! Why do you say no? Well, maybe Aladdin *is* rather fond of this old lamp . . .
Abanazar He'd be fonder still of a new one. (*Holding it up in front of her face*) All shiny and new—lovely—twinkle, twinkle, my dear!
Princess (*to the audience*) Shall I?
Audience NO!
Abanazar (*aside, with fury*) Yes, you blithering idiots, yes!
Audience NO!
Princess NO? Oh, I think it'll be all right, a new one will be a big surprise for my husband.
Abanazar It'll be a surprise all right, because—ZABUNDA! (*He snatches it from her, flings the cowl back, and waves the lamp*)

Horror from the Handmaidens

Princess (*screaming*) Aaaaaaah!

Abanazar rubs the lamp. There is a flash

> *The Genie enters*

Abanazar points to the Genie, speaking distinctly

Abanazar Make Aladdin's palace fly through the air!
        And take us to *Egypt*, take us there!

> *Abanazar and the Princess exit, he dragging her off*

The Genie waves his arms at the upstage palace on the hill. We hear a Swanee Whistle effect, there is thunder and lightning, and the palace rises from off the hill. Underneath it we see a Chinese style cloud and the cut out floats across the roofs of Pekin and exits

    The Chinese Police run on, blowing whistles and pointing to the sky

Bamboo The palace has gone!
Typhoo It's vamoosed!
Bamboo \ (*in an outer-space voice*) Unidentified Flying \ (*Speaking*
Typhoo / Object—U.F.O. . . .   / *together*)

    All except Widow Twankey, Aladdin, Wishee, Abanazar and the Princess, enter shouting and pointing in the air to where the palace has disappeared

All (*horrified, pointing upwards*) Egypt! It's flown to Egypt! Help! What will Aladdin do? Oh my daughter! See the palace flying away! To Egypt! This is fearful!

All point and gaze off with hands shielding their eyes and shouting

Black-Out

SCENE 2

THE STREET OF A THOUSAND CHOPSTICKS

Tabs or a front cloth of a Chinese street

Twankey, Wishee and Aladdin enter in their "poor" clothes from act I scene 1, or wear comedy tattered clothes, especially Twankey. They all three hold out their hands, begging

Wishee \ Penny for the guy! Penny for the guy! / (*Speaking*
Twankey /   \ *together*)
Aladdin Who's the guy?
Wishee \ You are. (*Calling*) Penny for the guy, / (*Speaking*
Twankey /   penny for the guy!   \ *together*)
Wishee (*comically depressed*) Oh it's so sad, so terribly sad. (*He looks off*) Hey, here are some Citizens! They'll give us some money!

    The Citizens of Pekin enter and cross the stage chatting animatedly to each other, completely ignoring the stretched out hands of the begging Twankeys, and exit again the other side

    One Boy and Girl stop C, gaze into each other's eyes and finally kiss. All this is watched romantically by the three Twankeys

Three Twankeys (*sentimentally*) Aaaaaah . . . (*Soon they say it again, only louder*) Aaaaaah . . . (*Remembering*) Penny for the guy, penny for the guy!

The two lovers ignore them

(*Sentiment gone, shouting*) Penny for the guy, penny for the guy!

The Boy and Girl exit dreamily, leaving the muttering and fed up Twankeys. The Vizier and Pekoe enter

The Twankeys renew their begging

Penny for the guy! Penny for the guy!
Pekoe (*indignantly*) Give money to *you*?
Wishee (*overacting like crazy*) But I haven't eaten for three days!
Vizier Well force yourself. Ha ha ha ha!

The Vizier and Pekoe laugh together. The three Twankeys are shocked and look at each other

Three Twankeys How rude!
Vizier Serves you right. The Princess should have married *my* son, then she wouldn't be in the mess she's in now.
Twankey No—she'd be in a worse one, married to Lord Muck over there!
Pekoe (*indignantly*) I'll have you know, my good woman, we have a *magnificent* family tree.
Wishee Yes—and you're the sap!

Pekoe reacts

Vizier Peasants! You should respect us, we're very upper class indeed.
Pekoe (*to the audience*) Yes, *we* live in—(*local snob district*)—and you can't do better than *that*, can you?

The audience react

   Pekoe and the Vizier exit haughtily

The three Twankeys, in time together, put their fingers to their noses and make raspberry noises at the departing pair

   The Emperor and Empress enter from the other side

Empress (*furiously, pointing to Aladdin*) This is disgraceful! Your palace went up in the air!
Emperor (*to the audience*) Yes, and what about the price of—(*topical item*). Everything's going up!
Aladdin Your Magnificence. I'll get the Princess back if it's the last thing I do.
Empress It will be if I have anything to do with it. (*Thunderously*) Come, Chopsuey!
Emperor Yes dear. (*He runs after her then turns back*) She's taking me to see (*topical film*). It's on at the Pekin Plaza. It's all about ...
Empress CHOPSUEY.
Emperor Coming, my little Chinese flower.

   The Emperor and Empress exit

Twankey takes out paper and starts to write on it

Twankey Well, here we are back to square one—we're broke!

Aladdin My palace has gone, my lamp has gone, my Princess has gone. What are we going to do?

Wishee We'll have to live off Pal Meat, and I know a way we could have one square meal a day!

Aladdin How?

Wishee Oxo cubes.

Aladdin Oh don't. Here, why is Mum so silent?

Wishee Yes, what you doing, Mum?

Twankey The Pools. You never know, we might win the Pools!

Aladdin What a good idea! (*He looks at the pools coupon Twankey is holding*) Chelsea and Oldham? They won't draw. And as for Middlesborough, they haven't won anything for six weeks!

Wishee You take my advice, put a nought by . . . (*He sticks out his bottom*)

Aladdin What's that mean?

Wishee Southend. (*To the audience*) Anyone that says Arsenal go home at once, *out*.

Twankey (*To Aladdin*) Which team do you fancy?

Aladdin sticks out his bottom, then shakes it

We've just had Southend.

Aladdin This isn't Southend, this is "Ips—twitch".

Twankey (*writing her pools*) Ipswich.

This routine can easily be made to include others in the cast if required (although it is only written for the three Twankeys here), starting as follows

(*Writes pools*) Ipswich. I don't know much about football.

Aladdin Well, we've got to win the pools, we're skint!

Wishee (*looking off*) Oh here's Typhoo and Bamboo!

The Chinese Police enter

Twankey Oh hello, you two, now Aladdin's palace has gone we're skint.

Aladdin We're trying to do the pools.

Typhoo Oh, we can help you, can't we, Bamboo?

Bamboo Oh yes! We'll show you all about honourable pools!

Aladdin runs off one side, Wishee runs off the other side and returns with an old motor-horn which he hoots

Twankey What team's that?

Wishee Tooting.

Twankey (*writing*) Tooting.

Wishee runs off his side. Aladdin returns with a cardboard cut-out of a gate which he holds above Twankey's head

Twankey What team's that?

Aladdin Gateshead.

Aladdin runs off

Twakney (*writing*) Gateshead.

Wishee runs on with a bra from the laundry scene

What's *that* got to do with football?
Wishee It's a good supporter.

*Wishee runs off his side, as Aladdin runs on with a blown up rubber glove
and a stool*

Aladdin Hold that, Mum.

*Twankey holds the glove, Aladdin sits on the stool and makes out he is
milking the glove*

Twankey What on earth's that?
Aladdin 'Uddersfield.

*Aladdin runs off. Wishee runs on holding a dog's lead, he trails it along
and talks to an imaginary dog*

Wishee That's it then—come on, nice walkies . . .
Twankey What team, please?
Wishee Leeds. Oh, and my dog will help you, he's got a lovely name:
Rover.
Twankey (*writing*) Rovers.

*Wishee runs off. Aladdin runs on with a child's spade, doing a digging
action*

And what team is that?
Aladdin Bury. Here's another team. (*He continues the digging motions,
makes clip clop noises and mimes riding a horse*)
Twankey And that?
Aladdin Canterbury.

Aladdin runs off, as Wishee runs on with a child's wheelbarrow

Twankey And that?
Wishee Barrow.

*Aladdin runs on with a cut-out of a man's face, it stops at the neck. He puts
it in the barrow*

Aladdin Wonderful Scots team.
Twankey What is?
Aladdin Ed—in—Barrow.

*Aladdin runs off, Wishee takes out a revolver and talks to an invisible
person*

Wishee Marnock, take *that*. (*He fires the gun at the invisible person*)
Twankey What team's that?
Wishee Kilmarnock.

Wishee runs off, taking the wheelbarrow with him, as Aladdin runs on with two baby dolls which he rocks to and fro

Twankey What's that team?
Aladdin Motherwell.
Twankey Oh I *knew* that was Motherwell.
Aladdin Well, if you knew that, Old—'Em. (*He dumps the two baby dolls on Twankey*)

Wishee runs on, talking to an imaginary person again

Wishee Take *that*. (*He fires the gun*)
Twankey I know that one. That's Kilmarnock.
Wishee No. It's Alder-shot.
Twankey I'm getting a bit confused.
Aladdin I think we better organize you, Mum. Now, have you got your teams down?
Twankey Yes
Wishee Have you got your homes down?
Twankey Yes.
Aladdin Have you got your aways down?
Twankey Yes.
Wishee Have you got your draws down?
Twankey *Oh, you filthy beast.* (*She hits Wishee and clutches at her skirts*) Now, I'll post off the pools—I might win!
Wishee I've just remembered. Villa's at home, Bromwich is away.
Aladdin *Bromwich* is away? My palace and my Princess—*they're* away! But where?
Twankey (*to the audience*) Anyone know where Aladdin's palace has gone?

The audience answer something

   To *Egypt?*
Audience Yes—to Egypt (*etc*)
Aladdin *Egypt?* Oh charming . . .
Wishee But how can we afford to go there? You'll have to sell your ring.
Aladdin What ring?
Twankey The one Abanazar gave you, you chump!
Aladdin Why, of course! (*He holds out his hand, showing the ring*)
Wishee Bit dirty isn't it? Here . . . (*He takes out a handkerchief and cleans the ring with it*)

Magic music is heard

The Oriental-looking Spirit of the Ring enters and poses stylistically, hands held in the Indian style

Wishee, Twankey and Aladdin are all admiring the ring and do not hear the magic music nor see the Spirit

Spirit Worry not! Be of good cheer!
          My master calls and I am here

The others realize that someone has joined the group

Wishee (*nudging*) It's the Avon Representative.

They all stare at the Spirit, who is a rather superior person

Spirit The Slave of the Magic Ring am I!
Aladdin And can you help us?
Spirit I can but try!
Aladdin Well, Abanazar's got the lamp, and my palace has flown away to Egypt!
Spirit I can fly you all to Egypt as quick as a flash!
Wishee (*explaining*) Perhaps she's Virgin!
Twankey (*scandalised*) What did you say?
Wishee Oh Mum, Virgin *Airlines*! (*To the Spirit*) P'raps you *can* help us?
Spirit Well I can guess where Abanazar will be. (*To Widow Twankey*) Do you know the Pyramids?
Twankey Of course—they're a pop group! Fabulous! Number Six in the charts.
Spirit (*witheringly*) They are ancient buildings in Egypt. Widow Twankey, prepare to take off.
Twankey (*alarmed, clutching on to her clothes*) Ay? Take off what?

The Spirit is dignified and sophisticated, and is becoming offended

Spirit Ladies and gentlemen, please don't scoff
Just follow me and we'll take off!
Twankey⎤
Wishee ⎬Sorry—apologies—beg your pardon ... ⎫(*Speaking*
Aladdin⎦   ⎬*together*)
Spirit Spirits of Mountain and Sea and Air
Take us to Egypt—takes us there!

The four of them loudly sing and hold out their arms as though imitating airplanes and the girl who flies in the commercial

All Four (*loudly*) "We'll take good care of you—fly the flag!!!"

And as they sing this, they start to shuffle off and exit, to a loud fanfare.

Blackout. In the darkness we hear a few bars of dramatic Oriental-style music, leading to the next scene

SCENE 3

THE ROOM OF MY MUMMY IN THE GREAT PYRAMID IN EGYPT

Sombre stone walls, but covered in bright orange, red, yellow and brown hieroglyphics—figures of Ancient Egyptians and stylized eagles, etc. Up C *is a large "block" and lying on it is a Mummy. In front of the Mummy's block is a stone bench. Standing up at each side of the bandaged Mummy are painted Mummy cases, such as may be seen in any museum. They are, in fact, practical doors—or can be simple cut outs touching the wings*

Seated on the bench in front of the Mummy, between the two painted Mummy cases, is Abanazar. He tenderly pats the lamp as he holds it. Standing in two diagonal lines at each side of him are Ancient Egyptian style or Arabian Style Slaves/Attendants. They are posed as though in an Egyptian frieze

Music starts, Abanazar speaks over it

Abanazar Here I am in the Great Pyramid! Next door is the treasure room and in it is the Princess, and gold galore! (*He laughs*) To think that all my life I've been saying "If only I could be rich!" (*He sings, or speaks to the music*)

SONG 11

The tempo of the song is such that after he has sung some of the number, the Slaves/Attendants can dance in an "Egyptian Frieze" sort of way

After the Production Number, two Slaves bring on the struggling Princess

My beloved! No-one will ever guess that the Genie has brought us to Egypt!

Princess (*looking round*) But why are we in *this* dismal place?

Abanazar They may find Aladdin's palace where it's landed, but they'll never ever find us here. Never!

Princess (*shuddering*) Inside the Great Pyramid!

Abanazar (*nodding*) I am an Egyptian, I love pyramids, I love the desert.

(*He sings unaccompanied*)
    "Blue heaven and you and I
    And sand kissing a moonlit . . ."

Princess You've got a frog in the throat!

Abanazar Sorry. (*He clears his throat, and continues*)
    "And sand kissing a moonlit sky
    The Desert breeze whispering a lull . . ."

Princess Now you've got a toad in the hole!

All the Slaves laugh

Abanazar Silence you scum. Get you gone! Imshi! Imshi!

The Slaves exit

Princess (*calling after them as they go*) Save me someone! Oh, Aladdin! *Aladdin!*

Abanazar You'll have to shout louder than that. Aladdin's in China and we're in Egypt.

Princess I was in Heaven and—(*defiantly*)—now I'm in hell!

Abanazar Oho—showing a bit of spirit, are we? But the best spirit of all is the spirit of the lamp!—and I've got it right here in my hand. (*He holds it up*) Yes, I'm Laurence Nightingale, the Man with the lamp!

Princess And what am I . . .?

Abanazar You'll be Mrs Abanazar when you marry me.
Princess (*gasping*) But you can't marry me, I'm married already!
Abanazar I'm not going to let a little thing like that get in my way.
Princess But that would be bigamy!
Abanazar Yes, my pretty, and you'll be bigamissis. Come, we must get ready for the marriage ceremony.
Princess You're depraved!
Abanazar Yes, isn't it *lovely*. (*He holds her hand and recites, holding the lamp on high with his other hand*)
> We'll be King and Queen of the Universe
> For me, for better—
> For you, for worse!

Abanazar drags the Princess off and both exit, she crying out and struggling

We hear the wind rushing effect and the Swanee Whistle sound

The Spirit of the Ring enters stylistically from the other side. She beckons in Twankey and Wishee—one or both in African Safari gear—and Aladdin. They gaze round uneasily

Comedy/spooky music plays

Spirit Behold—the Pyramid of my mummy!
Twankey Oh blimey, doesn't it look crummy!
Aladdin Is this where Abanazar
And my fair Princess have come?
Spirit It is indeed, oh Master,
And so my task is done!
If Bravery and Courage are combined
Your fair Princess you easily will find!

The Spirit bows stylistically with her hands held in the Indian style, and exits

Wishee (*frightened*) Hey! Come back! Don't leave us in here, it's scarey!
Twankey (*looking round and whispering mysteriously*) It's the Chamber of Horrors. (*Still whispering mysteriously*) Or is it an all-night sitting of Parliament . . .
Wishee (*suddenly calling out hysterically, his hands over his eyes*) I can't see, I can't see, I can't see!
Aladdin (*also hysterically*) Mother, he can't see!
Twankey (*also hysterically*) Oh my son, why can't you see?
Wishee I've got me eyes shut.
Aladdin Now cool it Wishee, cool it. (*Encouragingly*) You're *brave*. You're *brave*. What are you?
Wishee I'm frightened. (*He starts to cry*) I'm frightened and I want my Mummy!
Twankey (*pointing to it*) You've got him.
Wishee (*seeing it, and gasping in terror*) Ach—the Invisible Man! And he's wearing twenty five yards of Elastoplast!
Aladdin Now relax, you two, don't be frightened, it's just a perfectly

ordinary Egyptian Mummy so let's all have a jolly good laugh. Come on, on the command of three, one—two—three . . .

The three of them start to slowly and dismally laugh, then they gradually work themselves up into wild hilarity, clutching themselves with laughter. Then there is a loud sombre bell stroke heard from offstage. They freeze, and the laughter stops dead

Twankey (*eerily*) Time for din-dins!

A sombre voice is heard on the offstage microphone

Voice (*off*) Welcome to my room in the Pyramid of my Mummy.
The Three (*scared stiff*) Thank you very much. Very kind.
Voice Later on I want you to drink Egyptian wine in my chamber.
Twankey In your chamber? You must be joking!
Voice (*fading away*) Welcome to Egypt, to Egypt, to Egypt . . .
Twankey What was that?
Aladdin (*listening to the voice*) Perhaps it's the Sphinx.
Wishee Yes the smell's terrible.
Twankey He didn't say stinks, he said—(*close to Wishee's face*)—Spppppppinx.
Wishee (*wiping his face*) Let us spray.
Aladdin I said the *Sphinx*. I'm going to investigate. Who knows, there may be spirits about!

Aladdin exits

Twankey (*enthusiastically*) Spirits? Where? (*She looks round*) Ah, I see what he means! (*She picks up a bottle from near the Mummy and comes downstage again*) A nice drop of whisky!
Wishee (*still scared*) He means ghosts—he means the Mummy!
Twankey Oh, you're not scared of the Mummy! Let's have a bit of fun with it. You go up to it and prod it. (*She prods her finger in the air*)
Wishee (*terrified*) What?
Twankey Prod it! It won't bite you! If it does, bite it back!
Wishee (*gasping at this thought*) What? (*Recovering*) Well—all right . . .

Downstage, Twankey mimes having a nip of the whisky, though the bottle remains full, while Wishee runs up to the Mummy. From the side he gently prods it. To a loud ratchet sound from percussion the laid out Mummy slowly raises an arm and lowers it

Wishee registers comic horror, backs away and thus goes backwards into a secret panel—the first painted Mummy case—and disappears. Or he exits behind the cut out of a Mummy and into the wings

Twankey (*calling*) Anything happen dear? (*No reply*) Wishee? (*She turns round and looks*) He's vamoosed! (*She runs up and searches near the Mummy*) He's gone, where is he? (*She calls*) Wishee? Where are you Wishee? What's happened to the boy?

During this search she moves round in a circle and comes far down stage and faces right, searching

Wishee enters down L, *having moved round behind the scenery. He goes up to Twankey and taps her on the shoulder from behind*

(*jumping*) AAAAH!

At this she jerks the whisky bottle up in the air a couple of times and the contents—water—fly out over the front rows of the audience. They both see what she has done, and try not to laugh

(*To a girl in front row*) Oh! Oh dear! Well, it's only whisky, dear.

Wishee (*to Twankey*) What are you laughing at? (*He points to another girl*) You've drenched this lady! Look at her nice dress, you've ruined it!

Twankey (*to the second girl in the audience*) I am sorry love. Take it into Sketchleys—(*local cleaners*)—and send me the bill. You know where I live in Pekin—it's not far from—(*local place*).

Wishee (*to the audience*) Mum didn't mean it—it's her nerves. (*He laughs*) Silly to be frightened isn't it? I bet the Mummy hasn't been off that slab for two thousand years!

Twankey (*laughing*) Of course it hasn't dear!

They look out front as they chat to each other. The Mummy gets up and lumbers forward, to loud percussion boom—boom—boom footstep noises on the offstage microphone

Wishee (*laughing*) Still, I think I'd like a drink to keep me happy.

Twankey Here you are then.

The Mummy grabs the bottle from Twankey's outstretched hand. She moves her hand to give the bottle to Wishee, they both see there is nothing in her hand, look with alarm at the audience, slowly turn their heads and thus see the Mummy which is now directly behind them, hovering over them with its arms held up. They scream and clutch each other, maybe Wishee jumps upwards and Twankey catches him

Twankey ⎫
Wishee ⎬ AAAAAAH! ⎱ (*Yelling*
⎭   ⎰ *together*)

The Mummy waddles away and exits R *with the bottle, as Aladdin runs in from elsewhere*

Aladdin What's the matter?

Twankey ⎱ We thought Mummy was a dummy but ⎱ *Speaking*
Wishee ⎰   Mummy's *not* a dummy!   ⎰ *together*

Aladdin I don't know what you two are talking about. I told you to relax! Now come on, bring the bench down here and relax.

Aladdin organizes them, and they bring the bench downstage as he continues speaking

Now sit down, everything's going to be perfectly all right, my friends will help you. (*To the audience*) I know the Mummy won't come back but if it does, will you shout out "Mummy"?

Audience Yes!

Aladdin Great! That'll make Mum and Wishee feel much safer!

Wishee Singing a song always makes me feel safer.
Twankey Good idea. We'll sing the Mummy Song.

They sing, unaccompanied, a song about money, replacing the word "money"
with "Mummy"

SONG 11a *"The Mummy Song" (unaccompanied)*

The Mummy waddles in, waves the bottle threateningly at them, and exits
again through the Mummy case

Audience Mummy!
Wishee Mummy? Where?
Twankey Did you see the Mummy?
Audience Yes!

The three stand up, turn round, decide it is not there and sit down and sing
again

   The Mummy enters R

   Mummy!
The Three (*looking* L) Where? I can't see it!

   The Mummy hands Wishee the bottle and lumbers off, exiting R

Wishee (*casually*) Thanks. (*He realizes, freezes, his eyes popping*) Help!
   (*He looks round bewildered*) Someone's been and come and been and
   gone again!
Twankey They have? (*To the audience*) Then listen you lot, you must call
   out louder if it comes back!

   The Twankeys sing again. The Mummy enters behind them with a club,
   biffs each of them on the head with it—loud percussion "biff" noises—then
   waddles upstage and exist through the "door" of the first painted Mummy
   case, up R

The Three You hit me on the head—I did nothing of the sort—yes you
   did, I felt it—no I didn't (etc.)
Aladdin Stop arguing! We'd better look for it! (*To the audience*) Is it
   there? (*He points* L)
Audience No!
Twankey Is it there? (*She points* R)
Audience No!
Wishee Then is it *there*? (*He points upstage over his shoulder*)
Audience Yes!

They turn round

The Three Where is it then?
Audience Behind you! (etc.)

Obeying the audience shouts, they stand up and look for it

Wishee (*points to the first secret panel*) You mean here?
Audience Yes!

Aladdin Then we'll wait for it! Mum, you stand there. Wishee, you stand there, get ready for it and . . .

They group round the first Mummy case

> *The second case opens, and the Mummy stalks out, clubs Wishee on the head, and exits back into it*

The audience shouts advice

Wishee OW! (*He rubs his head*) Where is it? (*To the audience*) You mean it came out of *that* one? (*He points to the second Mummy case*)
Audience Yes!
Wishee (*to Aladdin*) It came out of *that* one! (*He points to the second Mummy case*)
Aladdin All right, we'll soon get this organized—come on!

Aladdin arranges Twankey, Wishee and himself by the second Mummy case, and they stand in a group at the side, waiting tensed for the Mummy to come out, arms held up ready to pounce on it

The Three This is it! We've got it now! At last!
Aladdin I'll open the door! Get ready—get set—*now*. (*He opens the door to the second case*)

> *Instead of the Mummy an impressive looking Ghost appears and hovers, arms held up high*

Ghost Voice (*blowing extremely loudly into the offstage microphone*) WHOOOOO!
The Three (*reacting with terror, as a sort of echo*) WHAAAAAA!

Vaudeville music as the Ghost chases them

> *Twankey, Wishee and Aladdin exit shouting loudly for help, followed by the howling ghost. Abanazar and the Princess return with the Chief Slave who carries a small table or stool. He or she places it* C

Abanazar (*to the Slave*) Prepare the room for our wedding.

The Slave bows and stands C, *with arms folded*

Princess You can't do this, you evil monster!
Abanazar Silence! The High Priest of the Pyramid will marry us.
Princess (*calling*) Aladdin! Save me Aladdin!
Abanazar Aladdin save you in the Middle East?
  He'll not interfere with our wedding feast!

He holds the lamp and laughs, and tries to embrace the Princess

  I don't need this lamp to see what I'm doing
  And it gets in the way of my billing and cooing.

He puts the lamp on the table or stool

Princess You wouldn't dare touch me if Aladdin were here!
Abanazar Well he isn't, so I will.

He tries to embrace her. She struggles and bites his hand

OW! She *bit* me!

The Slave (*announcing*) Make way for Aztok, the High Priest of the Pyramid!

Abanazar Aztok!

Two Slaves enter, each with cushions, and with ceremony put them on the floor each side of the table, and bow

(*to the Princess*) This will be quite painless. A simple Marriage Ceremony in the Ancient Egyptian style.

Princess You mean with handcuffs!

Abanazar (*offended*) Certainly not. Just these two prayer cushions, one on each side of the Table of Love.

The Slave (*looking upstage*) Here comes the Priest! (*To her*) You kneel there. (*To him*) You there oh master.

Sobbing, the Princess kneels on one cushion. The beaming Abanazar kneels on the other, and we hear fanfare and strange Egyptian music

All those at the opening of the scene enter with garlands and streamers or banners and arrange themselves by the table as though for the ceremony. Then the High Priest enters in a dark cloak wrapped around him, a large grey beard and a big turban or pointed hat

Abanazar (*bowing to the floor from his kneeling position*) Aztok! Aztok!

The Princess is sobbing. The High Priest pulls off his hat and beard, revealing the fact that he is Aladdin!

Aladdin Hello folks! It's me—and I've got the lamp! (*He grabs it off the table and waves it on high*)

Abanazar (*swaying in prayer*) Aztok—Aztok . . . (*Suddenly realizing*) No! I am betrayed!

Aladdin You stay down there, I don't trust you. (*To the audience*) What shall we do with him?

The audience shout "Murder him", etc., but the Princess moves to Aladdin

Princess Spare him. I know a *perfect* punishment!

Aladdin What's that?

Princess He's been evil all his life, let him be nice for a change!

Abanazar (*horrified*) No!

Aladdin Yes! (*He rubs the lamp*)

The Genie enters

Genie You command and I obey!

Aladdin Make the evil Abanazar *nice*.

Genie It shall be done! (*He makes magic passes at Abanazar*)

Abanazar No! Don't make me nice, I want to be nasty forever! (*With his usual evil laugh*) Ha ha ha . . . (*But the laugh suddenly stops as the Genie's spell hits him. He stands up and suddenly smiles sweetly and sings*) "All things bright and beautiful, all creatures great and small."

Abanazar goes and takes a bowl of rose petals from the nearest Slave Girl, sprinkles them in the air, and exits with a sickly smile

Aladdin turns to the Genie

Aladdin Take us from this Pyramid, dark and grey!
          Take us back to Pekin without delay!
Genie You command oh master—and I obey!

All raise their arms. We hear the Swanee Whistle and magic music

All (*in a shout*) PEKIN!

Blackout. The tabs close, or front cloth is lowered

SCENE 4

THE WILLOW PATTERN PLATE

Tabs, or one of the front cloths already used

Twankey enters in a different costume—a bright coloured comedy hat and smock style coat that can easily be changed for the finale walk down

Twankey So we're all back home in Pekin and everybody's happy! And there's only one thing left to do, and you'll NEVER GUESS what it is! I know it's a revolutionary idea, never been done before, but we're all going to sing a song! Yes, I heard the gasps of amazement! (*Calling off*) Bamboo, Typhoo! Bring on the Willow Pattern Plate, there's dears!
The Chinese Police wheel on a large circle of hardboard painted to look like the traditional blue and white Chinese Willow Patten Plate
(*Pointing to the design on it*) Now there are the lovers, there are the blue birds and what's she doing as she comes round the mountain? Ah, cue for song!

There is a mark on the edge of the plate to show the correct "top". It is now turned round and we see crazy Chinese characters on the other side

Right. Can you read Chinese?

The audience shout back

All right, then. We'll try a chorus!

All sing a chorus of "Coming Round the Mountain" which the audience will know

(*After it*) You got the words *right*. You can read Chinese! Give yourselves a clap!

She leads the audience into applause

You're so good you deserve a present. Let me think—I know! (*She goes to the magic plant*)
Audience Wishee!

Wishee runs on in a bright costume to be easily changed for the finale

Wishee Thanks, kids! (*To Twankey*) What were you doing, mucking about with my plant?

Twankey Well, our friends out there were so good!

Wishee Then why don't you ask them to sing with us up here? 'Cos you all know the song, don't you?

Twankey Yes—come on, kids!

Wishee I'll bring up on stage the best behaved ones.

Twankey You'll have difficulty finding any of *them* tonight!

Wishee (*laughing*) If any of you want to come up—five of you, please. That's it . . .

Five children from the audience come up on the stage. Wishee and Twankey arrange them in a line

Twankey (*to the children*) Are you having a good time?

Children Yes.

Twankey I'll soon put a stop to that. Now, when we tap you on the shoulder it's your turn to sing, so blow the roof off. Come on, number one, your time's up!

Twankey taps the first child on the shoulder, and the song divides into five lines of the lyric and then five of "Aye, aye, ippee ippee aye." Thus Twankey and Wishee travel down the line twice behind the children

Wishee (*after it*) That was brilliant! Now you'll be wondering why I asked you to look after my magic fruit tree all evening and I'll tell you. Very odd things grow on fruit trees—things like fruit gums.

Wishee takes, from the tree area or shelf, fruit gum packets and hands them out Twankey gets the audience to applaud the kids and helps them off the stage again. All sing the final chorus of the song sheet

    Twankey and Wishee wave good-bye and exit

    Grand Fanfare, the front cloth rises or the tabs open to show the final scene

SCENE 5

THE FEAST OF CHINESE LANTERNS

Perhaps Chinese bridge is at the upstage corner for the cast to enter over, using it as the Chinese version of the finale staircase. On the bridge and hanging from the flies are lit Chinese lanterns
If the scene starts choreographically, the first of the Chorus enter with lanters. All are singing

SONG 1 (reprise)

The song is followed by the Finale walk down, the last two being Aladdin and the Princess, greeted by a cheer from the cast, leading into the final couplets

Emperor   The Pantomime is over!
Empress   We've done the best we could!
Abanazar I know I was a baddie, but I'm going to be good!
Princess I'll never hear again the words "New Lamps for Old".
Twankey   And careful when you get outside, the—(*local place or street*)
              —is flippin' cold!
Wishee   Away to your Rolls Royce—but before you *do* decamp—
Aladdin   Good night, God bless—from Aladdin
              And his wonderful magic lamp!

Final chorus—

CURTAIN

FURNITURE AND PROPERTY LIST

NOTE: A "magic" pot with piece of plant showing in it remains on stage throughout the Pantomime

ACT I

SCENE 1

On stage: Pagoda-style buildings, obelisks
Various Chinese banners
Bench

Off stage: Scooters or skateboards (**Police**)
Large laundry basket (**Stage Management**)
Shopping or big bag of laundry (**Twankey**)
Basket. *In it:* packets of Tunes, Mars Bars, packets of crisps with one open (**Twankey**)
Scimitar (**Executioner**)
2 parasols (**Handmaidens**)
Coloured cardboard box (**Abanazar**)
Duplicate box containing flag (**Stage Management**)
Slate and chalk (**Abanazar's Assistant**)
Large coloured bottle (**Assistant**)
Blue cloth, stick with toy yacht (**Assistant**)
Toy revolver (**Assistant**)
Large envelope with card inscribed "NO" (**Assistant**)
Large envelope with photograph of baby (**Assistant**)
Bench, sticks with prop shoes (**Assistant**)
Large cloth (**Assistant**)
Trick cabinet (**Assistants**)
Book (**Vizier**)
Bag of laundry (**Aladdin**)
Axe (**Executioner**)
Small vest (**Wishee**)

Personal: **Bamboo:** whistle
Typhoo: whistle
Executioner: domino mask

SCENE 2

Off stage: Large bag or holdall. *In it:* fez (**Twankey**)

Personal: **Abanazar:** money

SCENE 3

On stage: Stagecloth (for later 'slosh')

Several "dly-cleaning" notices

4 tubs (see Production Notes)

> *In 1st tub:* packet of Tide, bright red underpants, small bra, 3-cup bra, soccer shirt, Victorian combinations, washboard, thimble
>
> *In 2nd tub:* blue bloomers, large bra, normal bra, soccer shirt with holes, corsets with padlock, washboard, thimble
>
> *In 3rd tub:* huge pair of underpants with hole, bright pink bra, large bra with 3 tennis balls sewn in, shirt with crown on flap, man's pants with padlock, washboard, thimble
>
> *In 4th tub:* large coloured bloomers, dark blue bra, tape with 1 large bra cup, dark blue shirt with stars, bloomers with 2 letters "D", washboard, thimble

Table. *On it:* laundry basket with hardboard replica of combinations, soda syphons, plastic buckets filled with coloured "slosh", 2 large flat plastic basins

Off stage: Trick battery and bulbs (**Fourth Citizen**)

Personal: **Twankey:** pad, pencil

               Princess: ring

SCENE 4

On stage: Rocks, one with heavy sliding door

Off stage: Pistol (**Vizier**)

Personal: **Musical Director:** pistol

SCENE 5A

On stage: Magic lamp on rock or shelf

Off stage: Torch (optional) (**Abanazar**)

               Spider (set in flies) (**Stage Management**)

SCENE 5B

On stage: Jewels, vases, chests of money

Off stage: Caskets of jewels (**Slave Girls**)

ACT II

SCENE 1

On stage: See Production Notes

Balustrade

Chinese banners and menu on walls

Several tables and chairs. *On tables:* dishes of food, glasses, napkins, chopsticks

Off stage: Trays of food (**Waitresses**)

Trick candle (**Wishee**)
"Red hot" poker (**Twankey**)
Jewels from previous scene (**Slave Girls**)
Cut-out barrel labelled "oil" (optional)·(**Slave Girls**)
Camera, tripod (**Madam Flash Bang**)
Ornamental chest. *In it:* various garments as dressing, magic lamp
    (**Handmaidens**)
Wooden rack of new lamps (**Abanazar**)

Personal: **Wishee:** large daisy buttonhole

Scene 2

Off stage: Motor horn (**Wishee**)
    Small cut-out of gate (**Aladdin**)
    Bra (**Wishee**)
    Blown-up rubber glove, stool (**Aladdin**)
    Dog's lead (**Wishee**)
    Child's spade (**Aladdin**)
    Child's wheelbarrow (**Wishee**)
    Cut-out of man's face (**Aladdin**)
    Revolver (**Wishee**)
    2 baby dolls (**Aladdin**)

Personal: **Twankey:** pools paper, pencil
    Wishee: handkerchief

Scene 3

On stage: Large block. *Beside it:* bottle of whisky
    Stone bench
    2 Mummy cases (in reality practical doors)

Off stage: Club (**Mummy**)
    Small table or stool (**Chief Slave**)
    Cushion (**Slaves**)
    Garlands, streamers, banners (**Crowd**)
    Bowl of rose petals (**Slave Girl**)

Scene 4

Off stage: Hardboard circle—Willow Pattern plate (**Police**)
    Near magic tree: packets of fruit gums

Scene 5

On stage: Chinese bridge
    Chinese lanterns

Off stage: Chinese lanterns (**Chorus**)

LIGHTING PLOT

Property fittings required: strings of Chinese lanterns
Various front cloth and full stage settings

PROLOGUE (*optional*)

To open:	Light on Abanazar	
Cue 1a	As **Spirit** enters *Spot on Spirit*	(Page x)
Cue 1b	Abanazar and Spirit wave their hands *Lightning*	(Page xi)

ACT I

To open:	Full stage exterior lighting	
Cue 1	**Abanazar:** "Kalakazoom!" *Flash in footlights*	(Page 8)
Cue 2	**Vizier:** "Ow!" *Black-out, then up to front cloth lighting*	(Page 16)
Cue 3	As Scene 3 opens *Bring up full stage lighting, interior*	(Page 21)
Cue 4	**Wishee:** "Night Time, Please!" *Black-out*	(Page 23)
Cue 5	After **Fourth Citizen** works torch trick *Revert to previous lighting*	(Page 23)
Cue 6	**Abanazar:** ". . . and confusion reign!" *Flickering Strobe lighting—continue until end of chase*	(Page 28)
Cue 7	As tabs close *Cross-fade to front stage lighting—exterior, mysterious*	(Page 29)
Cue 8	**Emperor's** trousers fall *Black-out, then immediately up to previous lighting*	(Page 31)
Cue 9	**Abanazar:** "Ha ha ha ha ha ha" *Black-out, then fade up to single glow on magic lamp as tabs open—and general dim, shadowy lighting as Scene 5A opens*	(Page 33)
Cue 10	**Aladdin** rubs lamp *Flash*	(Page 35)
Cue 11	**Genie:** "Hidden in the magic cave!" . . . rocks part *Dazzling, glittering lighting on jewels, etc.*	(Page 35)

ACT II

To open:	Full stage lighting	
Cue 12	**Genie** enters *Bring up green spot on* **Genie**	(Page 40)
Cue 13	As chase enters auditorium *House Lights up: fade as* **Abanazar** *returns to stage*	(Page 41)
Cue 14	**Twankey:** "Well, strike me pink!" *Black-out. Pink spot on* **Twankey**. *Fade spot and return* *to previous lighting as she exits*	(Page 41)
Cue 15	**Genie** makes magic pass at **Wishee** *Flash*	(Page 41)
Cue 16	**Genie** exits *Flash, fade green spot*	(Page 42)
Cue 17	**Genie** exits *Flash*	(Page 43)
Cue 18	**Abanazar** rubs lamp *Flash*	(Page 46)
Cue 19	**Genie** waves arms at palace *Lightning*	(Page 46)
Cue 20	As crowd shout and point off *Black-out, then up to front stage lighting*	(Page 47)
Cue 21	The **Twankeys** shuffle off *Black-out, then up to full, slightly eerie stage lighting*	(Page 52)
Cue 22	**All:** "PEKIN!" *Black-out, then up to front stage lighting*	(Page 60)
Cue 23	As Scene changes *Full stage lighting, with lanterns, for Finale*	(Page 61)

EFFECTS PLOT

PROLOGUE (*optional*)

MADE AND PRINTED IN GREAT BRITAIN BY
LATIMER TREND & COMPANY LTD PLYMOUTH

MADE IN ENGLAND